CRYPTORUNES

Codes and Secret Writing

Clifford A. Pickover

SAN FRANCISCO

This book is dedicated to

ᛏᚻᛖ ᛗᛋᚠᚻᚻᚨᚷᚢᛋ ᚹᛁᛏᚻᛁᚾ ᚨᛚᛚ ᚩᚠ ᚢᛋ.

Acknowledgments

I owe a special debt of gratitude to my wonderful illustrators, who designed the exotic symbols used in this book: Michael H. Lee, Josh Dixon, Daniel Steven Smith, Curtis Clark, Morten Bek, David F. Nalle, Professor Odd Einar Haugen from the Department for Nordic Studies at the University of Bergen, Martin Bergman, Alan Carr, Cosmonaut Fonts, and Poul Steen Larsen. Jeremy T. Teitelbaum provided some information on letter frequencies. I thank Diego Doval, Marsha Sisolak, David Glass, Paul Berliner, and Brian Mansfield for advice and encouragement.

Martin Gardner's *Codes, Ciphers, and Secret Writing* (Dover, 1972) is a fine introduction to secret codes of all kinds. David Kahn's *Codebreakers* (Scribner, 1996) is the recognized bible on the history of secret communications from ancient times to the Internet. Fred Wrixon's *Codes, Ciphers and Other Cryptic and Clandestine Communications* (Black Dog & Leventhal, 1998) also provides useful background information. Some of the topics discussed in chapter 3 are also considered in my book *The Science of Aliens* (Basic Books, 1998). Jennifer Smith's website The Runic Journey (www.tarahill.com/runes/) provides excellent historical information on runes.

Published by
Pomegranate Communications, Inc.
Box 6099, Rohnert Park, CA 94927
www.pomegranate.com

Pomegranate Europe Ltd.
Fullbridge House, Fullbridge
Maldon, Essex CM9 4LE, England

Library of Congress Cataloging-in-Publication Data

Pickover, Clifford A.
Cryptorunes : codes and secret writing / Clifford A. Pickover.
p. cm.
ISBN 0-7649-1251-8
1. Cryptography. 2. Cryptography—Problems, exercises, etc. 3. Runes. I. Title.
Z103 .P5 2000
652'.8—dc21 99-049288

Cover and interior design by Wind Design, Mill Valley, California

Printed in U.S.A.

09 08 07 06 05 04 03 02 01 10 9 8 7 6 5 4 3 2

CONTENTS

Introduction

— 11:6

The strange-looking codes in this book come from another world—an ancient world filled with sticklike runes, a beautiful alphabet used by Northern Europeans from the first century A.D. into the Middle Ages. In this book, they serve as portals to secret knowledge and provide an exquisite puzzle experience.

Does your mind wander when you think through a problem at home, school, or work? Instead of making creative jumps, are you often confronted with mental blocks? Perhaps your brain needs a little exercise, a bit of extra conditioning. *Cryptorunes* is a book for anyone who wants a mental workout—to increase attention span, to improve memory, and to stretch the imagination.

Runes are everywhere these days. English novelist J. R. R. Tolkien featured runes in his epic trilogy *The Lord of the Rings*. These odd symbols are in New Age shops selling fortune-telling paraphernalia; they're featured in religious rituals; they're even worn as jewelry. In fact, runes are a big business. Companies offer "rune-reading courses" so that students can become "certified rune masters." The Lost Mountain Trading Company of California sells rune sets containing semiprecious stones and carrying bags. Tara Hill Designs of Ontario, Canada, supplies handcrafted wooden rune sets and other Norse-related products. More than fifty books dealing with rune magic and divination are in print. Jennifer Smith, author of *RAIDO: The Runic Journey,* notes:

> Today, runes have been rediscovered as a symbolic system and have gained immense popularity as a means of divination. They are, however, much more than a curious alternative to Tarot cards for telling fortunes. They provide a key to understanding the lives and beliefs of the ancient people who created them, and have much to teach us about a way of life that was perhaps more intimately connected to the natural world, and to the realm of spirit, than our own.

What Are Runes?

Runes were used by Germanic peoples of northern Europe, Britain, Scandinavia, and Iceland until the sixteenth or seventeenth century. The runes served as both a written alphabet and a set of symbols used for magic and divination. Runes faded from use when Roman alphabets became the preferred script of most Europeans, but some forms and meanings of runes were preserved in inscriptions and manuscripts.

The primary characteristic that distinguishes a runic alphabet from the English alphabet is that each letter, or rune, has a meaning. For example, whereas "ay," "bee," and "cee" are meaningless sounds denoting the first three letters in English, the names of the first three runes, *fehu* (ᚠ), *uruz* (ᚢ), and *þurisaz* (ᚦ) are actual words in the Germanic language, meaning "cattle," "aurochs" (a wild ox, now extinct), and "giant," respectively. Runes were thought to have mystical significance; thus, the simple process of writing may have been transformed into a magical act.

Because runes consist of angular letter forms and because early runic inscriptions were written from right to left like the earliest alphabets, some people believe that the runic alphabet came from a more ancient system, perhaps even the Greek or Latin alphabets a few centuries before Christ. Another theory is that the Goths (a Germanic people) developed the runic alphabet from northern Italy's Etruscan alphabet, and the runes may have been further influenced by the Latin alphabet in the first or second century B.C.

It's not necessary to know the history of runes to embark on the mysteries in *Cryptorunes;* however, just a smidgen of background may deepen your appreciation for these exotic symbols.

There are at least three main varieties of runic script:

- *Early* forms (also known as Common, Germanic, or Teutonic), used in northern Europe before A.D. 800. This script had twenty-four letters. The sounds of the first six letters were *f, u, th, a, r,* and *k,* giving the alphabet its name: *futhark.* The earliest runic forms seem to be written both left to right and right to left, with no distinction between uppercase and lowercase letters.
- *Anglo-Saxon,* or Anglian, forms, used in Britain from the fifth to the twelfth century A.D. This script had twenty-eight letters to accommodate additional sounds, and after A.D. 900 it had thirty-three letters. The letter shapes were slightly different from those of the Early forms.
- *Nordic,* or Scandinavian, forms, used from the eighth to the thirteenth century A.D. in Scandinavia and Iceland. In Scandinavia, runes were still used for charms and memorial inscriptions until the seventeenth century. (The number of futhark runes was reduced to sixteen; several different Scandinavian sounds were represented by a single rune.)

Other varieties of runes included three variants of Nordic script: the *Hälsinge Runes,* the *Manx Runes,* and the *stungnar runir,* or "dotted runes." More than 4,000 runic inscriptions and several runic manuscripts are still available today for researchers to study. Approximately 2,500 of these come from Sweden. Others come from Denmark, the Schleswig region of Germany, Britain, Iceland, various islands off the coast of Britain and Scandinavia, France, Ukraine, and Russia.

Ogham, created by the Celts, is another fascinating and cryptic alphabet; it has been categorized as Primitive Irish. Some historians suggest that ogham was a private code used by the Druids, the often secretive Celtic religious group from Britain, France, and Ireland. Ogham dates from A.D. 350 to 600 and has been found on stones in Ireland and the Isle of Man. Ogham looks like groupings of lines:

Centuries ago, runes were inscribed on everything from coffins to coins, and were sometimes sanctioned by the Catholic Church. Many people knew simple runic spells and consulted runes on questions of public and private interest. In 1639, the church banned the use of runes as part of its drive to rid Europe of the devil. Some rune masters were killed. Others hid. Much rune knowledge was lost.

Perhaps the queerest episode in the history of runes was their use by German scholars connected with the Nazi movement in the 1920s and 1930s. What began as a legitimate interest in ancient folklore became so intertwined with Nazi ideology and racism that the German research shed little light on the true origin and meaning of runes.

After the Second World War, rune studies were discouraged because of their association with Nazism, and very little was written about runes until the 1950s and 1960s. J. R. R. Tolkien stirred interest in runes with his best-selling novels on Middle Earth, which often contained pictures and descriptions of runes. Tolkien was not just a fantasy writer; he was also a professor of Anglo-Saxon (Old English), English language and literature, and philology (historical linguistics) at the University of Oxford. Tolkien was particularly interested in the relationship of Anglo-Saxon to linguistically similar languages (Old Norse, Old German, and Gothic), with emphasis on the dialects of Mercia, that part of England in which he lived. He was also interested in Middle English and the dialect used in the *Ancrene Wisse,* a twelfth-century manuscript probably composed in western England.

Anyone reading Tolkien's *Lord of the Rings* or reading about Tolkien's life could not help but become interested in runes. But many who had never heard of Tolkien became excited by runes in the 1980s, when popular New Age trends and a revival of pagan religions (especially the Asatru movement dedicated to ancient northern European, pre-Christian religions) helped runes regain their popularity as a divination system and as symbols of an ancient, forgotten people.

When I began my search for drawings and photos of ancient runes, I was delighted to find historical runic inscriptions on objects ranging from swords to stones to bronze pendants. These examples listed the entire runic alphabet in order. The only surviving written accounts of the names and meanings of the runes, however, were not recorded until the ninth century. These rune poems have a verse for each rune, each of which begins with the rune itself and its name. The rune names are thought to be accurate, although no manuscript exists listing the names of the older, Germanic runes. Runes have been called cryptic because their origins are uncertain and because runes were used as a concealment system. Their original angular shapes (for example, ᚠᚢᚦᚺᛗ ᚠᚷᚺᛁᚼᛃᛚᛗᚼᚠᛈᛉᚱᛋᛏᚢᚹᛉᚦ) with no curved lines may indicate that the first writing implements that created them were wooden sticks or bones.

Should You Read This Book?

Although this book uses runes and other odd symbols, from ogham to Mycenaean Linear B, it is really a book on cryptography—the science of secret writing. You'll use the book to try decoding cryptic messages using rules that cryptographers have used from ancient to modern times. Get ready for lots of mystical thoughts, such as:

ᛏᚼᛁ ᚼᛁᛏᛏᛁᚾ ᚼᛁᚱᛉᛏᚾᛦ ᛁᛋ
ᛒᛁᛏᛏᛁᚱ ᛏᚼᛁᚾ ᛏᚼᛁ ᛏᛒᚢᛁᛏᚢᛋ ᛏᚾᛁ.*

Confused? That's part of the fun. There's a trick. In order to understand the wise messages, you've got to solve a challenging cryptogram. There are dozens of cryptogram books on the market, but in *Cryptorunes,* unlike the others, you're going to have a mystical quest and challenge. By substituting a rune for each English letter, I have transformed the quotations and sources—from poet Kahlil Gibran to psychologist R. D. Laing—into brain-crushing puzzles. Clues and solutions are given at the end of the book.

For the ultimate challenge, I offer clues about the locations of several marvelous golden runes in chapter 5, "The Golden Rune Contest." This is a challenging cryptographic adventure: can you decode the clues and find the strange locations of the mysterious golden runes?

This book is for anyone who wants to enter new mental worlds and solve puzzles—students, behaviorists, psychologists, educators, cryptographers, computer programmers, CIA agents, NSA directors . . . Teachers may want to use the cryptic designs to intrigue their students. Students may design their own codes similar to the ones in this book. Computer programmers may create or solve cryptorunes using a computer, although a computer is definitely not necessary to attack the problems in this book.

When I talk to students about the secret codes in this book, they are always fascinated to learn that they can break the codes using a little logic, a few rules, and common sense. The codes can be explored with just a pencil and paper. Anyone can be an amateur cryptoruneologist.

Work in teams. If you are a teacher, have cryptorune codebreaking contests to see which team of your students can find the solutions first. As students solve the cryptorunes and read some of the accompanying material, not only will they have great fun and learn to focus on symbolic problems, but they'll also be learning a lot about the structure of language and the history of codebreaking. Chapters 1 and 2 give codebreaking hints and simple examples to explain how to make your own secret messages and how to crack other people's.

THIS BOOK IS ORGANIZED so that you can jump right into a cryptorune and have fun, without having to sort through a lot of cryptographic background. The book is not intended for cryptographers looking for formal mathematical explanations or a wide coverage of different cryptographic methods. Some hints are repeated so that you can choose a cryptorune to solve at random.

To some extent, I chose cryptorunes for inclusion in this book arbitrarily, but I was also seeking to give a nice introduction to some common problems in cryptography. I designed these cryptorunes myself and have received mail from readers about them. Many are representative of a wider class of problems of interest to cryptographers today. The cryptorunes vary in difficulty, so you are free to browse. A few are awesomely difficult for secret reasons, but most are quite approachable.

* The hidden harmony is better than the obvious one.

Prepare yourself for a strange journey as *Cryptorunes* unlocks the doors of your imagination. Each cryptorune is a world of paradox and mystery. Grab a pencil. Do not fear. The cryptorunes may appear to be curiosities, with little practical application or purpose. However, I have found these experiments to be both useful and educational—as have the many students, educators, Tolkien fans, and scientists who have written to me. To encourage your interest and enjoyment, I provide a range of designs and clues. Seeing a clue or solution at the end of the book will sometimes clarify a method and encourage you to try another code.

Think of this book as a mental ocean. As you surf, each strange-looking puzzle exercises your eye and mind. Enjoy the cryptic waters. Be careful not to get caught in the undertow. Take deep breaths. Don't stay in too long. Let your mind rest between puzzles.

How the Book Is Organized

This book is divided into five chapters:

1. "Cryptography": a brief introduction to simple codes and secret writing.
2. "How to Crack Cryptorunes": a set of instructions for solving cryptorunes. These rules deal with the structure of the English language and can also be used for solving other people's codes in which a symbol stands for an English letter.
3. "Secret Codes from the Stars": an exploration of what you could do if you received a message in an alien language. Would you be able to decode it?
4. "Cryptorunes": Mystical quotations, along with their authors' names and sources. I have converted these into cryptorunes, with each rune or other symbol standing for an English letter. (Some cryptorunes are more difficult because more than one English letter is represented by the same rune.) Although each quotation has its own code, within that quotation the same rune substitutions are used.
5. "The Golden Rune Contest": clues, hidden deep within a set of puzzles, for finding several mysterious (fictional) golden runes. I don't give you the solutions or any other clues, except for coded clues within the "visitations." Can you be the first to win the contest and find all of the runes? See the special prize offer in this section.
6. "Clues": a separate chapter, before the chapter that gives cryptorune solutions, to offer you one clue, or letter equivalent, for each of the cryptorunes. Since each puzzle has its own code, each puzzle will have a different clue. The clue gives your brain a start, but it won't make the cryptorune too easy to solve.
7. "Solutions": the decoded quotation for each cryptorune.

Chapter 1

CRYPTOGRAPHY

Mercury Rising and the Navajos

In the 1998 movie *Mercury Rising*, Bruce Willis plays an FBI agent trying to save an autistic boy from a vile government plot. Nine-year-old Simon Lynch is not just autistic, he's also a savant, capable of solving impossibly intricate puzzles just by looking at them. Unfortunately for Simon, he is able to crack a supposedly unbreakable new security code called Mercury. As a result of his peculiar talent, Simon becomes the target of a National Security Agency operative. The agency's secret formula was put inside a common puzzle magazine to test whether any brainy geeks could detect the code. Once Simon dials the encrypted phone number that only his perceptive eyes can see, his parents are eliminated by an assassin, and Simon himself must flee for his life.

Does this plot sound far-fetched? Cryptography, the writing and deciphering of messages in secret code, has played an important role in the history of every nation and is essential today for our country's security. In fact, all governments and spies need to send special information in secret codes, and many nations need a staff of expert, full-time cryptanalysts working to crack the codes used by friendly and enemy nations.

Humans have created codes to keep secrets since the time of the Pharaohs. For millennia, wars have been fought between code makers and code breakers, and the stories of these skirmishes are humankind's secret history. From Julius Caesar's Gallic Wars to our modern-day Desert Storm operation in the Persian Gulf, codes have shaped the course of our history to an extent we can hardly fathom.

During World War II, in Great Britain alone 30,000 people were assigned to break codes. Today the United States has tens of thousands of code breakers, collaborating with computers, costing us more than $1 billion a year. The U.S. 1942 victory at Midway Island resulted from our breaking Japan's Purple Machine code. Germany's 1943 U-boat victories against the Allies resulted from Germany's breaking the British merchant ship code.

One of the most important solutions of a single coded message occurred during World War I when the British broke the German code called 0075, which promised Mexico a piece of United States territory if Mexico supported Germany in the war. This coded message made Congress and the American public so angry that our country declared war on Germany.

During World War II, Navajo Indians were used to transmit messages in their native tongue. From 1942 to 1945, the Navajo "code talkers" took part in every U.S. marine assault in the Pacific. They served in all six marine divisions, marine raider battalions, and marine parachute units, transmitting Navajo messages by telephone and radio—a code that the Japanese never broke.

The idea to use the Navajo language for secure communications came from Philip Johnston, the son of a missionary to the Navajos and one of the few non-Navajos who spoke their language fluently. Johnston had been reared on a Navajo reservation and was a World War I veteran who knew of the military's search for an unbreakable code. He also knew that Native American languages—notably Choctaw—had been used in World War I to encode messages.

Johnston believed Navajo was the ultimate code because it is a very complex, unwritten language. Its syntax and tonal qualities make it unintelligible to anyone without extensive exposure and training. It has no alphabet or symbols, and is spoken only on the Navajo lands of the American Southwest. At the outbreak of World War II, fewer than thirty non-Navajos, none of them Japanese, could understand the language.

During the war, Navajo code talkers transmitted information on tactics, troop movements, orders, and other vital battlefield communications over telephones and radios. They also acted as messengers and performed general marine duties.

At Iwo Jima, Major Howard Connor, Fifth Marine Division signal officer, declared, "Were it not for the Navajos, the Marines would never have taken Iwo Jima." Connor had six Navajo code talkers working day and night during the first two days of the battle. Those six sent and received over 800 messages, all without error.

The Japanese, who were skilled code breakers, remained baffled by the Navajo language. The Japanese chief of intelligence, Lieutenant General Seizo Arisue, said that, while they were able to decipher U.S. Army and Army Air Corps codes, they never cracked the code used by the marines.

When a Navajo code talker received a message, he heard only a string of unrelated Navajo words. The code talker first had to translate each Navajo word into its English equivalent. Then he used only the first letter of the English equivalent in spelling an English word. Thus, the Navajo words "wol-la-chee" (ant), "be-la-sana" (apple) and "tse-nill" (axe) all stood for the letter "a." If you wanted to send the message "The aliens have landed" using a similar approach in English, you could say:

> Teflon hangs early. Albert leaves insectivores each Nostradamus Saturday. Helmets are vaulting elephants. Liquid arsenic nears Damascus each day.

This kind of code can work beautifully for hiding messages from your friends. In fact they might never even guess the message was a code. But this approach would be too simple for the U.S. military to use. However, using Navajo is a different story. One way to say the word "navy" in Navajo code is "tsah (needle) wol-la-chee (ant) ah-keh-di-glini (victor) tsah-ah-dzoh (yucca)." How many people could crack *that* code?

More recently, codes were essential for maintaining the sanity of American prisoners of war. Although totally isolated from one another in the dreaded Hanoi Hilton during the Vietnam War, the imprisoned soldiers would tap codes to one another through the walls. The North Vietnamese never mastered the code, which arranged the alphabet on a five-by-five grid (omitting K, for which C was used). The prisoners indicated the row and column for each letter. For example, the letter C would be tap, pause, tap tap tap, because C was in the first row and third column. The code worked so well that at times the Hanoi Hilton sounded as if it housed manic woodpeckers. The prisoners told jokes to one another, and every Sunday they tapped out the Lord's Prayer in code.

What Is a Code?

In this book I use the word *code* rather loosely. There are many definitions of it. In one definition, a code is a rule for replacing a piece of information, such as a letter or word, with another object. A code doesn't have to be a secret known only to the sender and receiver of a message. For example, if you use a computer, you are using the most widely known code used today—the American Standard Code for Information Interchange (ASCII). It's used in all personal computers and represents 128 characters and operations (such as backspace). Specifically, ASCII characters are represented in the form of seven-bit binary numbers—a string of seven ones and zeros. In ASCII, a lowercase *a* is always 1100001, an uppercase *A* always 1000001; a *b* is 11100010, a *B*, 01000010; and so on. In fact, the ASCII code is not a bad one for you and your friends to use for sending secret messages, so long as you don't think your enemies know about ASCII codes. For example, if you had an ASCII conversion chart, you would know what this bawdy message means:

010001100 11001111 01011001 11001111
01010101 11001100 11001001 01001011
11000101 11010100 01001000 11000101
01010011 01010000 11001001 11000011
11000101 01000111 11001001 11010010
11001100 01010011?

Imagine how tricky this would be for your enemies to decode if you left no spaces between letters. You could take it a step further and replace the zeros and ones with symbols:

🗀🗁🗀🗀🗀🗁🗀🗀 🗁🗁🗀🗀🗁🗁🗁🗁 🗀🗁🗀🗁🗁🗀🗀🗁
🗁🗁🗀🗀🗁🗁🗁🗁 🗀🗁🗀🗁🗀🗁🗀🗁 🗁🗁🗀🗀🗁🗁🗀🗀
🗁🗁🗀🗀🗁🗀🗀🗁 🗀🗁🗀🗀🗁🗀🗁🗁 🗁🗁🗀🗀🗀🗁🗀🗁
🗁🗁🗀🗁🗀🗁🗀🗀 🗀🗁🗀🗀🗁🗀🗀🗀 🗁🗁🗀🗀🗀🗁🗀🗁
🗀🗁🗀🗁🗀🗀🗁🗁 🗀🗁🗀🗁🗀🗀🗀🗀 🗁🗁🗀🗀🗁🗀🗀🗁
🗁🗁🗀🗀🗀🗀🗁🗁 🗁🗁🗀🗀🗀🗁🗀🗁 🗀🗁🗀🗀🗀🗁🗁🗁
🗁🗁🗀🗀🗁🗀🗀🗁 🗁🗁🗀🗁🗀🗀🗁🗀 🗁🗁🗀🗀🗁🗁🗀🗀
🗀🗁🗀🗁🗀🗀🗁🗁?

Isn't that a dandy?

Professional cryptographers often restrict the word *code* to secret writing in which entire words, phrases, or syllables are replaced by other code words or code numbers, listed in a special codebook containing words in the original message (called plaintext). A portion of a true code might look like this:

codenumber	plaintext
1531	aardvark
2513	abacus
1432	abandon
5511	abattoir
1431	abbreviate
5987	I
1225	love

```
1738    you
3891    Monica
8722    Bill
```

This means that "1431" replaces the word abbreviate. Isn't this a fine way to send secret love letters to your sweetheart? Wouldn't spies have a hard time figuring out what "5987 1225 1738" really meant? The code would be fairly difficult to crack, but the major problem is that both you and the receiving person would have to make a list of words beforehand and consult the list when decoding the steamy, romantic messages. You wouldn't want other people to find your codebooks.

You can see from this example that a code consists of a gigantic cipher alphabet, in which the plaintext unit is the word or phrase. In ciphers, on the other hand, the basic unit is the letter. However, in this book, I will follow the common practice of using *code* as another word for *cipher*.

Ciphers, like codes, replace a piece of information with another object. Unlike a code, a cipher always implies deliberate secrecy. For example, ciphers replace symbols according to a rule defined by a secret key known only to the transmitter and the receiver, so that no one else can decrypt the cipher. Ciphers were crucial to the survival of advanced Arab civilizations and flourished in the seventh century A.D. The ancient Greeks and Romans often used ciphers to keep messages secret. Charlemagne, king of the Franks and founder of the Holy Roman Empire in A.D. 800, used exotic symbols (not unlike cryptorunes) as alphabet replacements in correspondence with his generals. In the Middle Ages, Catholic Church officials used ciphers.

Cipher making was common in the 1800s with the advent of telegraphy, because codebooks were vulnerable to capture during battle. In the twentieth century, machines were invented that could rapidly and electronically shuffle letters to create concealments of fantastic complexity.

Why care about such subtle distinctions between codes and ciphers? One reason is that today information is frequently both encoded and encrypted. For example, a satellite communications link may encode information in ASCII characters. It then encrypts the resulting coded data into ciphers by using a "Data Encryption Standard." Finally, the cipher stream itself is encoded again, using codes for transmission from the ground station to a satellite. These operations are undone, in reverse order, by the intended receiver to recover the original information.

You may wonder if you have any personal involvement with cryptography. But most of us depend on it for protection. Do you use a credit card? The personal identity number (PIN) that you enter into an automated teller machine (ATM) is stored in the bank's computers in an encrypted form (as a cipher) or is encrypted on the card itself. Similarly, communications between the ATM and the bank's central computer are encrypted to prevent thieves from tapping the phone lines and recording the signals that make the ATM cough up your cash.

Cryptography also prevents forgers from counterfeiting winning lottery tickets. Each ticket has two numbers printed on it: the identifying number announced when a winner is sel-ected, and an encrypted version of this number. This means that a counterfeiter can't print a forgery when the winning number is announced unless the crook has also figured out the lottery's cryptosystem.

There are many other examples of the role cryptography plays in our everyday lives. It protects electronic mail and the databases in which personal tax, income, medical, credit rating, and other related data are stored. Cryptographic protection is essential to our basic freedoms. The United States recently recognized the danger to national security posed by computer system break-ins and telecommunications eavesdropping. To prepare for these situations, National Security Directive 145, implemented in 1984, established a National Telecommunications and Information Systems Security Committee, which provides telephone and computer security for the federal government and its contractors. With the explosive growth of the Internet and the access it provides to business and personal records, we must constantly use cryptography to protect ourselves. Information theft is one of the major problems faced by our computer-centric society, and it touches every aspect of private and commercial life.

Ciphertext and Plaintext

Encryption is the process of disguising a message or text so that its meaning will not be apparent to anyone who may intercept it, accidentally or otherwise. In this book you'll work mostly with a simple encryption procedure called a substitution cipher, in which each letter of the original message (the plaintext) is replaced by a rune to generate the coded message (the ciphertext).

One of the simplest and oldest substitution ciphers is one created by writing the alphabet forward, and then, underneath, writing the alphabet backward (figure 1). Each letter stands for the letter directly below. A message such as "The aliens are among us" would be written:

```
Gsv zorvmh ziv znlmt fh.
```

Notice that this would be more difficult to decode if you grouped the letters in triplets:

```
Gsv zor vmh ziv znl mtf h.
```

The reverse alphabet cipher is too risky to keep your diary in. It is so well known that your enemies, competitors, spouse, parents, girlfriends, boyfriends, employers, and in-laws might be able to figure it out too quickly. However, it takes only a little more effort to make the cipher more difficult. For example, just by changing the mapping of letters every paragraph, the code becomes much more difficult to crack. You can imagine many more tricks. As mentioned, you can regroup letters in pairs, triplets, or quadruplets—or you might leave no spaces at all between letters. You could map the cipher to a backwards message, so that all words, once deciphered, had to be spelled backwards to arrive at the original message. Or you could scramble the message in other ways. You could occasionally be redundant so that letters such as *u* and *v* might map to the same coded symbol. You could remove punctuation marks.

Julius Caesar encrypted his military field reports by replacing each letter of the Latin alphabet with the letter three characters farther down the list, "wrapped around" by repeating the alphabet after the letter z. Try to send your friends ciphers with this approach. All you have to do is agree on a secret key—for example, six. Write the alphabet in a row. Put your finger on *a* and count six letters to the right, starting on *b* and ending on *g*. Put *a* above *g*. Continue to the right with *b*, *c*, *d*, until you reach *z* on the line below, and then go back to the beginning and finish the alphabet. Your six-shift cipher can be represented as in figure 2.

To encode a message, find the letter in the top row and substitute for it the letter below. For example, each letter in *north* shifts forward seven letters to become *tuxzn*. Make sure you

Plaintext letters:	a	b	c	d	e	f	g	h	i	j	k	l	m	n	o	p	q	r	s	t	u	v	w	x	y	z
Cipher letters:	z	y	x	w	v	u	t	s	r	q	p	o	n	m	l	k	j	i	h	g	f	e	d	c	b	a

fig. 1

Plaintext letters:	u	v	w	x	y	z	a	b	c	d	e	f	g	h	i	j	k	l	m	n	o	p	q	r	s	t
Cipher letters:	a	b	c	d	e	f	g	h	i	j	k	l	m	n	o	p	q	r	s	t	u	v	w	x	y	z

fig. 2

don't give anyone your key, six, or that person will be able to decode your message easily. Imagine how tricky it would be to decode your message if the key kept changing for each sentence. For example, you could create a code based on 1492, the year Christopher Columbus landed in the Western Hemisphere: your first sentence would use a key of 1, the next sentence a key of 4, and so forth. You can keep recycling 1, 4, 9, 2, 1, 4, 9, 2, until the message is finished.

Coded messages are fun to encipher (put in cipher form) and decipher (translate back to the original). Mary, Queen of Scotland from 1542 to 1567, used ciphers to protect her correspondence. Many famous presidents, authors, and celebrities have kept parts of their diaries in code. For example, when Franklin Delano Roosevelt was twenty-one, he used a cipher for several diary entries. In 1971, these entries were shown for the first time to several cryptographers, who had no trouble breaking the code. It was a simple substitution code using numbers for vowels and symbols for consonants. I'm told that the translations were so bland that the code breakers wondered why young Roosevelt felt the need to encode them. I would be interested in hearing from any readers who know what the coded entries referred to.

Let's return to the cryptorunes in this book. If you are clever and hardworking, you can learn how to break almost all of the ciphers. If you don't think so, realize that solving substitution ciphers is now popular with enough fans to support a daily cryptogram puzzle in newspapers throughout the world.

Many substitution ciphers are known as *monoalphabetic* (or single alphabet). There are several definitions of monoalphabetic ciphers. One suggests that for every letter, one and only one letter (or symbol) is substituted. If the code letter for *a* is z, then whenever there is a z in the ciphertext, it means *a*, and no other letters in the text mean *a*. (Broader definitions suggest that, as long as only one cipher alphabet is used, the system is monoalphabetic or monalphabetic, even if a letter is replaced by any one of several symbols.) However, when two or more cipher alphabets are used in some kind of prearranged pattern, the system becomes polyalphabetic. Some authors define ciphers as polyalphabetic when different symbols in the ciphertext can stand for the same letter of plaintext, and the same symbol in the ciphertext can stand for different letters of plaintext.

A few of the cryptorunes have a redundancy in which more than one letter in the original text is assigned the same symbol in the coded message. For example, if the letters *x* and *y* in the plaintext are both represented by the letter *a* in the cipher text, the code breaking becomes slightly more difficult, but most words are obvious when decrypted because of their context and spelling. If the letter e and the letter *i* are mapped to the same symbol in the ciphertext, your friend expecting the message could understand it despite the fact that there is ambiguity about when the symbol stands for e and when it stands for *i*. You no doubt can figure out the meaning of the following even if you assign all occurrences of *i* to *e*:

```
Thi Russian submarini will attack
Niw York at fivi o'clock p.m.
```

Other Substitution Codes

In this book, you will encounter substitution codes using animals, buildings, alien-looking symbols, and runes, alphabets similar to ones used centuries ago in Scandinavia and Northern Europe. For example, "The aliens are among us" might be coded as

where the letter *t* is represented by , the letter *a* is represented by , and so forth. Notice that the decoding is made more difficult by the fact that the letter *l* is represented by the same symbol as the letter *a*. Even with this polyalphabetic cipher, if you had a few sentences to work with, you could probably soon decipher the message. This interesting detective work is explained in the next chapter.

During the American Civil War, Confederate soldiers used a visually interesting cipher called the pigpen cipher. (It is also known as the Masons' cipher because the Society of Freemasons used it more than a hundred years ago for secret messages. The Rosicrucians, a worldwide brotherhood claiming to possess esoteric wisdom handed down from ancient times, have also used this kind of cipher.) The cipher got the name "pigpen" from the way in which letters are separated by lines, like pigs in a pen. Each letter is represented by a series of fences (lines) and pigs (dots). A message is encoded by substituting for each letter a tiny drawing of the fences and dots.

The pigpen code is quite easy to use. First you write out the whole alphabet in two grids, as shown in figure 3. Each letter is represented by the part of the "pigpen" that surrounds it. If it's the second letter in the compartment, then it has a dot in the middle (*i* is represented by a box, and *j* is a box with a dot, for example). Can you decode the message in figure 4? (Hint: The last

AB	CD	EF
GH	IJ	KL
MN	OP	QR

ST
UV WX
YZ

fig. 3

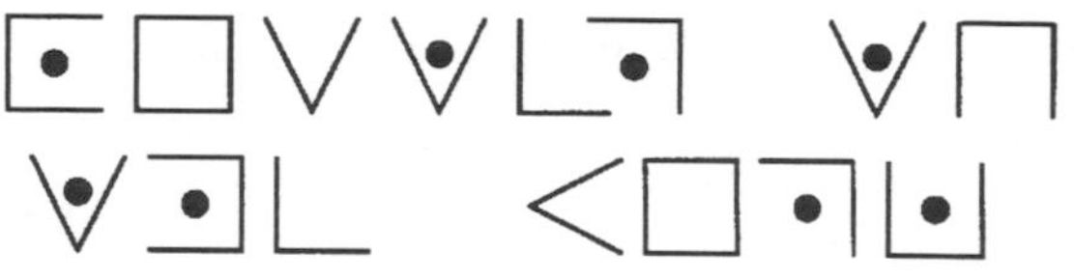

fig. 4

word is "wind.") If you want to use the pigpen code, you may wish to scramble the letters differently from the grid shown in figure 3 to make the code more difficult to break. For example, I've seen pigpen ciphers with the letters arranged as shown in figure 5.

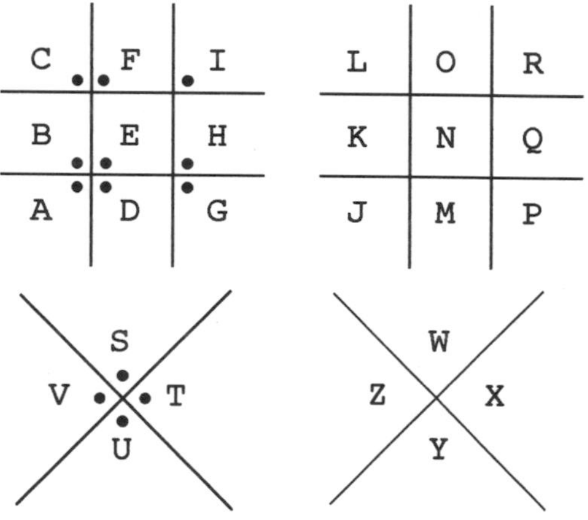

fig. 5

Figure 6 is an actual letter sent by a Confederate agent in 1863 and intercepted by the Union secretary of war. Part of the letter makes use of the pigpen cipher. The entire cipher required about four hours to decode; its message concerned a shipment of rifles.

American short story writer Edgar Allan Poe had an intense interest in cryptography and believed that he could break any cipher. In

December 1839, Poe issued a famous challenge in *Alexander's Weekly Messenger* stating that he could solve any simple substitution cipher that magazine readers submitted:

> It would be by no means a labor lost to show how great a degree of rigid method enters into enigma-guessing. This may sound oddly; but it is not more strange than the well known fact that rules really exist, by means of which it is easy to decipher any species of hieroglyphical writing—that is to say writing where, in place of alphabetical letters, any kind of marks are made use of at random. For example, in place of A put % or any other arbitrary character—in place of B, a *, etc., etc. Let an entire alphabet be made in this manner, and then let this alphabet be used in any piece of writing. This writing can be read by means of a proper method. Let this be put to the test. Let any one address us a letter in this way, and we pledge ourselves to read it forthwith—however unusual or arbitrary may be the characters employed. (C. S. Brigham, *Edgar Allan Poe's Contributions to Alexander's Weekly Messenger* [Worcester, MA: American Antiquarian Society, 1943].)

Poe insisted that each letter in the ciphertext correspond to one letter in the plaintext and that the cryptograms preserve the word boundaries by showing the proper spaces between words. Once you become good at solving the cryptorunes in this book, return to this chapter and try solving this cryptogram that a reader sent to Poe:

```
C'WW WPB VKI WPYKIY UN BI VKONJ
C'WW NZV BI VU VKI XIEB DZCNJ
PFL WPJI BI YVPEV
IPNK AUWWB YKPWW EINIOXI MB YVCFL
IPNK UCNI ZFVU MB AIIV CWW GECFL
PFL MPJI CV YMPEV.
```

Between December 1839 and May 1840, Poe apparently solved all the ciphers submitted to *Alexander's*. He claimed that "Out of, perhaps, one hundred ciphers altogether received, there was only one which we did not immediately succeed in solving. This one we demonstrated to be an imposition—that is to say we fully proved it a jargon of random characters, having no meaning whatsoever."

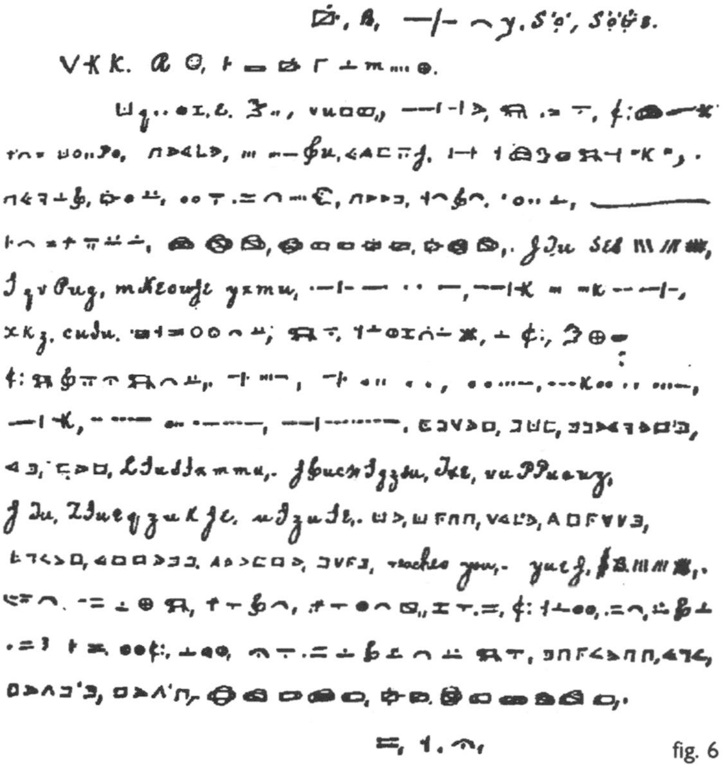

fig. 6

Poe also appears to have solved a cipher in which some symbols stood for more than one letter of the plaintext and a cipher in which seven different alphabets were used. We don't have an example of this latter ciphertext itself, but perhaps a new alphabet was used on each line of the plaintext. Poe reiterated, "We say again deliberately that human ingenuity cannot concoct a cipher which human ingenuity cannot resolve."

Edgar Allan Poe used a substitution cipher himself in his popular tale "The Gold Bug" (figure 7). The ciphertext was supposedly written by the pirate Captain Kidd, using invisible ink on a parchment. Word divisions were not indicated. The message, which tells where a treasure is buried, is:

```
5 3 ‡ ‡ † 3 0 5 ) ) 6 * ; 4 8 2 6 ) 4 ‡ .
) 4 ‡ ) ; 8 0 6 * ; 4 8 † 8 ¶ 6 0 ) ) 8 5
; 1 ‡ ( ; : ‡ * 8 † 8 3 ( 8 8 ) 5 * † ; 4 6
( ; 8 8 * 9 6 * ? ; 8 ) * ‡ ( ; 4 8 5 ) ; 5
* † 2 : * ‡ ( ; 4 9 5 6 * 2 ( 5 * - 4 ) 8 ¶
8 * ; 4 0 6 9 2 8 5 ) ; ) 6 † 8 ) 4 ‡ ‡ ; 1
( ‡ 9 ; 4 8 0 8 1 ; 8 : 8 ‡ 1 ; 4 8 † 8 5
; 4 ) 4 8 5 † 5 2 8 8 0 6 * 8 1 ( ‡ 9 ; 4 8
; ( 8 8 ; 4 ( ‡ ? 3 4 ; 4 8 ) 4 ‡ ; 1 6 1
; : 1 8 8 ; ‡ ? ;
```

fig. 7

A good glass in the bishop's hostel in the devil's seat—forty-one degrees and thirteen minutes—northeast and by north main branch seventh limb east side—shoot from the left eye of the death's-head—a bee-line from the tree through the shot fifty feet out.

In the story, Poe restates his assertion of code-breaking skill:

I have solved others of an abstruseness ten thousand times greater. Circumstances, and a certain bias of mind, have led me to take interest in such riddles, and it may well be doubted whether human ingenuity can construct an enigma of the kind which human ingenuity may not, by proper application, resolve. In fact, having once established connected and legible characters, I scarcely gave a thought to the mere difficulty of developing their import.

In Sir Arthur Conan Doyle's 1903 story "The Dancing Men," Sherlock Holmes encounters a cipher composed of stick figures. He determines that each word is terminated by the insertion of a little flag in the hand of the last "man" of each word. All spacing between words is omitted.

"Why, Holmes, it is a child's drawing," cried Dr. Watson when he first saw the figures on a torn piece of paper.

"It is certainly rather a curious production," said Holmes. "At first sight it would appear to be some childish prank. It consists of a number of absurd little figures dancing across the paper upon which they are drawn. Why should you attribute any importance to so grotesque an object?"

The distinctly human characters in *Cryptorunes* are based upon the secret alphabet developed by the gang of American criminals in "The Dancing Men." As Holmes deduces, the puzzle was actually a simple substitution cipher.

The story documents only seventeen of the twenty-six letters in the English alphabet, and this led to speculation about the full alphabet. Several essays and articles on the subject appeared in the specialist journals. About twenty-five years ago, a leading Danish Sherlockian, Aage Rieck Sørensen, privately published the definitive analysis of this obscure alphabet, including his derivation of the missing men.

When Sherlock Holmes finally figures out the code, he is able to reveal to Dr. Watson that the message

translates to "Am here Abe Slaney." (It turns out that Abe Slaney is "the most dangerous crook in Chicago" and is writing threatening notes in this cipher to a former childhood sweetheart.)

"I am fairly familiar with all forms of secret writing," Holmes declared, "and am myself the author of a trifling monograph on the subject, in which I analyze one hundred and sixty separate ciphers."

Wouldn't it be fun to write your own secret messages using the dancing man code? Written in this cipher, the first few lines of Genesis would be:

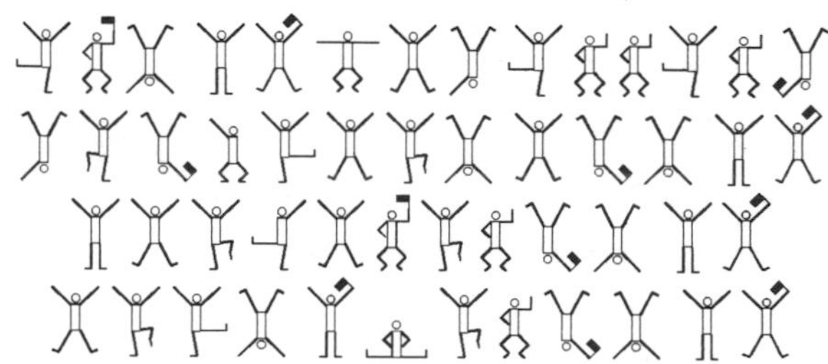

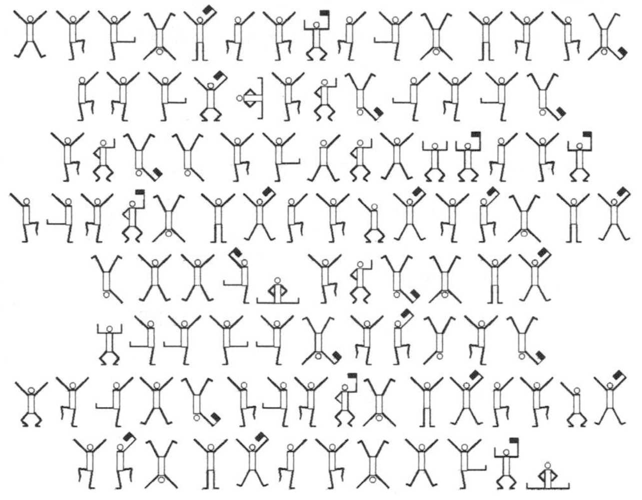

Can you decode the following statement by Jesus?

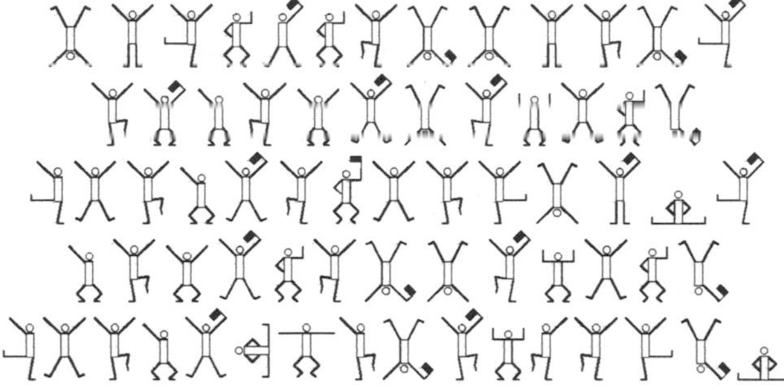

The literary genius Geoffrey Chaucer (1343–1400), author of the famous *Canterbury Tales*, also used ciphers in his work. Figure 8 shows a cryptogram from his book *The Equatorie of the Planetis* (1393), which describes the workings of an astronomical instrument. I do not know why he felt the need to encrypt the simplified directions for using the instrument. (Today, there is a little controversy about whether the *Equatorie* is really the work of Chaucer or of some contemporary.)

The *Equatorie* includes six passages written in cipher. The cipher system consists of a substitution alphabet of symbols. For example, *a* is represented by a symbol resembling a capital V. The solution to the cryptogram in figure 8 is: "This table servith for to entre in to the table of equacion of the mone on either side."

Future spies might need a degree in molecular

fig. 8

biology to keep up with secret codes devised by scientists. Researchers at the Mount Sinai School of Medicine in New York, for example, have placed codes within DNA, the hereditary molecule of living cells. The encryption technique is called steganography, because it conceals a message within a large number of similar objects. This means you wouldn't even know there was a secret message waiting to be found. In particular, the first step in the process of performing molecular steganography is hiding the message in the DNA and the second step is hiding the existence of the DNA by shrinking it to a small dot and putting it in an innocuous letter, like the O right here on this page. In 1999, researchers proved that the secret-message DNA worked by encoding the phrase "June 6 invasion: Normandy." The recipient used standard biochemical techniques to detect and read the secret DNA message.

Secret codes have even been used in attempts to prove the existence of life after death. In 1948, British psychologist Robert Henry Thouless created a "Vigenere" cipher code message:

```
BTYRR OOFLH KCDXK FWPCZ KTADR
GFHKA HTYXO ALZUP PYPVF AYMMF
          SDLR UVUB
```

A secret two-word key permits the decoding of the line, and only Thouless knew the code. He reasoned that if someone could break the code after he died, it would prove the existence of an afterlife because Thouless would attempt to transmit the code from the "other side." When

Thouless died in 1984, he took the key with him to the grave. Despite many attempts by spirit mediums to contact him, no one has succeeded in decoding the message.

Pig Latin and Anagrams

You can make your own ciphers more difficult to crack by first converting the English text to pig Latin before converting it to runes or any other set of symbols. Pig Latin is a novelty code language that has been around for many years and is used by children. Although a simple cipher, pig Latin takes a little practice to speak and read with ease. The rules vary slightly from place to place, but the basics are:

1. If a word begins with a consonant, the first letter is moved to the end of the word, and *ay* is added. Example: The word *magic* becomes *agicmay*.
2. If a word begins with a vowel, *way* is added to the end of the word. Thus *and* becomes *and-way*. (Some regional dialects of pig Latin add *ay*, *yay*, or *hay* to words with initial vowels.)

Some pig Latin speakers use a more complicated rule for 2:

2a. If a word begins with a vowel, the first letter is moved to the end, and *ey* is added. Example: The word *anchor* would become *nchoraey*.

2b. Exception to rule 2a: if the initial vowel is an *e*, use *ay* instead of *ey* at the end. Example: The word *elevator* becomes *levatoreay*.

3. For hyphenated compounds, some pig Latin fans prefer treating each part of the word separately. Example: The combination *next-door* becomes *extnay-oorday*.
4. Some pig Latin dialects move entire initial-consonant clusters. For example, *string* might become *ingstray* rather than *tringsay*.

> Using pig Latin, the first words of the Bible become: "In-way e-thay eginning-bay od-gay eated-cray e-thay eavens-hay and-way e-thay earth-way."

I have not been able to find the origin of pig Latin. Similar kinds of spoken jargon are practiced by children around the world from every culture. One purpose of pig Latin is to shield children's messages from the prying ears of adults. Oddly enough, male-female speech differences are apparent in many languages, perhaps so that males and females may shield their speech from one another. In the Mayrinax dialect of Atayal in northern Taiwan, women's speech is historically a more conservative variety, and men's speech shows unpredictable changes in pronunciation resulting from adding syllables to earlier word forms. In Tagalog and some other Philippine languages, adolescents conceal their messages with "backward speech." This sort of trickery is similar to English pig Latin. Iban of northwestern Borneo contains many words with reversals of the meanings found in corresponding words in other languages. Perhaps this reflects an earlier effort to disguise speech; it may have evolved into a language with altered meanings for all speakers.

Another obfuscation that can be used as a code is the anagram, a word or phrase made by transposing the letters of another word or phrase. In the 1992 movie *Sneakers*, Robert Redford leads a team that tests the vulnerability of security systems. One day his group is employed to acquire a black box that can crack any known encryption, which would give ultimate power to any government possessing it. In the movie, the box is used to tap into computer systems, including those of the government, the air traffic control system, state power grids, and other important agencies and infrastructure components. Everyone wants the box—our National Security Administration, the Russians, the Mafia.

While Redford ponders the mystery of the box, he comes across a company name, Setec Astronomy, which he determines is an anagram:

`Setec Astronomy = Too Many Secrets`

Redford is soon fighting for his life when the box falls into the hands of the wrong people.

Consider another famous anagram from my book *The Alien IQ Test*. Aliens have coded a message for humanity by scrambling an English sentence. On a cold October day, they descend to Earth in a yellow spacecraft and drop a titanium tablet on the barn of a Kansas millworker. The tablet contains scrambled letters. The message reads:

`Prowl cove open`

The farmer begins to place the letters in different orders in an attempt to descramble the message. Day and night he writes words on his barn in chalk. He continues to search for English words using the same letters as in the original message, but so far all the combinations have yielded nonsensical sentences—for example:

Nerve coop plow;
vowel prone cop;
colon prove pew;
clone prop wove;
propel cone vow;
copper love own

Even after a week, he cannot decode the message, and he fears for his family. Can you help him decode the message? Perhaps the aliens are telling us why they are colonizing our planet. Perhaps they are telling us about their food preferences.

This is a fun puzzle on which to end this chapter. The solution is given at the beginning of chapter 7. No reader has ever solved this.

CHAPTER 2
HOW TO CRACK CRYPTORUNES

Using this book, you can become the next Jean Champollion, the decipherer of ancient Egypt's hieroglyphics. Who knows, someday you may even help to decode a message from the stars, as I discuss in chapter 3. By solving the cryptorunes in chapter 5, "The Golden Rune Contest," you will learn the fate of the universe, the fate of humanity, the very nature of God, and the reason we are all here. Well, not exactly—but you may win a wonderful prize.

Solving cryptorunes quickly is an art that requires some knowledge and experience. In this chapter, I will give a few tips and show how you can solve the cryptorunes in this book. The most important hints deal with facts about the English language:

- The most often-used letter is e, followed in order by *t, a, o, i, n, s, h, r, d, l, u*. (E is also the most common letter in many other European languages, such as Spanish, Italian, French, and German.) This means that if you find one cipher (for example, ᚠ) more than any other in a particular cryptorune, there's a fair chance it stands for the letter e.
- The most common beginning letter of a word is *T*.
- The most common letter at the end of a word is e.
- A single-letter word is *a* or *I*.
- The most frequent two-letter word is *of*, followed by *to* and *in*. Other common two-letter words are *is, an, on, by, be, it,* and *or*.
- The most common three-letter word is *the*. The next most common is *and*. Other common three-letter words are: *you, are, any, but, not,* and *can*. If a three-letter word has double letters it is probably *all, too,* or see.
- Certain consonants occur together, such as *th, wh, sh,* and *ch*.

- The sequence of letters at the end of a word may indicate common endings such as *tion, ent, ant, ing, s,* or *ed*.
- *Q* is always followed by *u*.
- The consonant that most often follows a vowel is *n*.
- Quotations generally end with the name of the person quoted.
- The most common double letters are, in order of frequency, *ll, ee, ss, oo, tt, ff, rr, nn, pp*, and *cc*. Double letters usually can't be *aa, hh, ii, jj, qq, uu, vv, ww, xx*, or *yy*. Only extremely rarely do you find words with *kk*, such as "bookkeeper," which also happens to be the only word I know with three doubles in a row.
- A single cipher after an apostrophe (') probably stands for *s*, but it could also be *t* (as in *isn't*) or *m* (as in *I'm*). Also look out for *'ve, 'll*, and *'re*.
- The most frequently occurring four-letter word is *that*.
- Look for patterns. For example, *that* ends and starts with the same letter, so a pattern like ᚺᛒᚲᚺ is probably *that*. ᛒᛗᚲᚳᚲ is probably *there* or *where* or *these*. ᚺᛒᚲᛗᛒ is probably *which*. ᚺᛒᛒ might be *all, see*, or *too*.
- If you are stuck, read the clue in chapter 6 and let your mind fill in the blanks. English sentences and paragraphs often have a recognizable "flow" consisting of "someone doing something," with descriptive or qualifying phrases rounding out the picture.

The frequency with which the individual letters of the alphabet occur in samples of English text is an identifying characteristic of English. The order of frequency, from greatest to least, generally is *e, t, a, o, i, n, s, h, r, d, l, u, c, p, f, m, w, y, b, g, v, k, q, x, j, z*. Of course, individual texts deviate somewhat from this order. The tables below show the letter frequencies in a number of selected text samples (a frequency of 0.13 indicates that e, for example, occurs 13 times in every 100 letters). Certain combinations of pairs of letters (digrams) are also much more common than others. The ten most common digrams in each of the texts is also indicated.

The Book of Psalms (King James Version)

e	0.13	t	0.10	h	0.09	o	0.08
a	0.07	i	0.06	s	0.06	n	0.06
r	0.06	l	0.05	d	0.04	m	0.03
u	0.03	f	0.02	y	0.02	g	0.02
w	0.02	c	0.02	p	0.02	b	0.01
v	0.01	k	0.01	j	0.00	q	0.00
x	0.00	z	0.00				

Digrams: *th, he, an, in, ha, or, nd, re, er, et, ea, ou*

Unix Manual, page on the "printf" command

t	0.11	n	0.10	i	0.10	e	0.09
r	0.08	a	0.07	s	0.07	o	0.06
p	0.05	f	0.04	h	0.04	c	0.03
u	0.03	d	0.03	g	0.02	m	0.02
l	0.02	y	0.01	v	0.01	w	0.01
x	0.01	b	0.00	k	0.00	z	0.00
j	0.00	q	0.00				

Digrams: *th, in, he, er, nt, on, re, ar, te, ed, ri, st*

Encyclopedia Britannica, page on "Cryptography"

e	0.10	i	0.09	t	0.08	n	0.07
o	0.07	a	0.07	r	0.06	s	0.05
c	0.05	h	0.04	l	0.04	d	0.04
p	0.03	m	0.03	y	0.03	f	0.03
g	0.03	u	0.02	b	0.02	w	0.01
v	0.01	k	0.01	x	0.01	q	0.00
z	0.00	j	0.00				

Digrams: *in, th, ti, on, an, he, al, er, to, or, cr, si*

I have also analyzed the first few hundred words of some recent best-sellers and ranked single letters together with pairs of letters in order of frequency. I included blank spaces in this analysis, and the underscore symbol indicates a blank space. For example, e_, the first digram in each list, indicates that the most common digram in all of these books was e followed by a space. Note the remarkable similarities and several differences, such as the *o* ranked second in *The Millionaire Next Door: The Surprising Secrets of America's Wealthy*.

Stephen King's *Bag of Bones*:
e, t, a, o, n, h, s, r, i, d, l, e_, he, _t, u, th, e_, he _t, u, th, w, d_, _a

Tom Clancy's *Rainbox Six*:
e, t, a, o, n, i, h, s, r, d, l, e_, _t, th, he, w, u, _a, g, d_, t_, ., y, f, m

John Grisham's *Street Lawyer*:
e, t, a, o, n, i, h, s, r, d, l, e_, _t, he, d_, th, u, w, _a, m, c, t_, g

Tom Stanley and Will Danko's *Millionaire Next Door: The Surprising Secrets of America's Wealthy*:
e, o, t, a, n, i, r, s, h, l, e_, u, d, c, m, f, _a, _o, th, s_, w, _t, y, p, er, ., t_, in, on

Cliff Pickover's *Science of Aliens*:
e, t, i, o, a, n, s, r, h, l, d, c, u, e_, f, th, s_, _t, m, p, he, _a, n_, y, in, d_, g, an, er

To prepare you for the cryptorunes, let's practice by decoding a mystical quotation from a thirteenth-century Icelandic saga:

[runes] [runes] [runes] [runes] [runes] [runes] [runes] [runes] [runes] [runes] [runes] [runes] [runes]. [runes] [runes] [runes] [runes], [runes] [runes] [runes] [runes] [runes] [runes] [runes] [runes] [runes] [runes] [runes] [runes].

The cryptorune is fairly short, so we may not be able to rely on the fact that the most common letter in English is e. A good starting point is the third word, [runes]. Take a look at it. Have any idea what it might be? Its beginning and ending runes are the same. Recall that the most common four-letter word is *that*. Let's try substituting the letters *t, h,* and *a* for the corresponding symbols in this four-rune word and everywhere else those symbols are used:

[runes] [runes] that [runes] [runes] [runes] th[rune] [runes] t[runes] [runes] [runes] [runes] [runes]t[rune]. [runes] [runes] th[rune] [runes]a[rune], a[rune] [runes] t[rune] [runes] [runes] th[rune] [runes] [rune]h[runes] [runes] a[runes] [runes].

Our decoding seems to be going well; the seventh word, *th*[rune], is almost certainly *the*, giving us the e symbol, and *a*[runes] is therefore *are*. We can also see that *t*[rune] is *to*. Since we now know that [rune] is *o*, we can guess that the two-letter word [runes] is not the commonly used *of* but rather *in*.

So far we know the symbols for *t, h, a, r, e, o, i,* and *n*. The single-letter word starting the sentence is *I*. Let's give it all a try. Here's what we have so far:

I [rune]NO[rune] that I h[rune]n[rune] in the [rune]in[rune]X tree [rune]or nine [runes] ni[rune]ht[rune]. [rune]o[rune]n[rune]e[rune] [runes] the [rune]ear, an o[rune]erin[rune] to [runes]e[rune] on the tree [rune]ho[rune]e root[rune] are [rune]n[rune]no[rune]n.

Look how close we are to solving the thirteenth-century mystery! What else can we guess at this point?

Well, [rune]no[rune] is probably *know*; [rune]or is probably *for*. This means that `o`ᚳᚳ`erin`ᛘ is *offering*; `root`ᚻ is probably *roots*. With a little more analysis and guesswork, we finally decode the mysterious Icelandic quote:

> I know that I hung in the windy tree for nine full nights. Wounded by the spear, an offering to myself on the tree whose roots are unknown.

This example should give you a general idea of how to solve the cryptorunes that follow. Cracking the cryptorune codes is great fun—it gives you a thrill similar to that of a scientist or archaeologist discovering the workings of our universe, and the more codes you solve, the better you will get. Martin Gardner, in his book *Codes, Ciphers, and Secret Writings*, notes:

> The famous German philosopher and mathematician Gottfried Wilhelm Leibnitz once observed that solving a cryptogram is very much like solving a problem in science. If a scientist has only two or three unrelated facts about nature that need to be explained by a theory, he can usually think of dozens of equally good theories, just as a cryptographer can think of dozens of solutions for one short word. But if there are a large number of facts to be explained, it is like having a long cryptogram to solve. It is not so easy to invent one theory to explain hundreds of different facts which were previously mysterious. When such a theory is invented, and it fits all these facts, it is probably correct for a reason that is curiously similar to the reason why a solution to a long cryptogram is probably correct if it fits all the symbols.

Claude E. Shannon—an American mathematician who founded a branch of mathematics called communication theory—wrote an important paper ("Communication Theory of Secrecy Systems," *Bell System Technical Journal* 28 [October 1949]: 656–715), in which he showed that if a cryptogram has thirty or more letters, it is almost certain to have only one solution. But if it has twenty or fewer letters, it is usually possible to find more than one solution. The results in Shannon's paper grew out of his wartime work. After the Second World War ended, the work was declassified, possibly by mistake.

I asked some friends to attempt to solve a few cryptorunes. Later, when I interviewed them, my friends said that the runes were frustrating to work with initially. They could simplify the puzzles by first replacing the runes with English letters; however, most respondents reported that, after working with several puzzles, their minds snapped into gear and became comfortable working with the runes.

Good luck on your quest. Remember that, if you have a sufficiently long piece of text, a monoalphabetic substitution cipher can be broken by comparing the relative letter frequencies in the ciphertext with the corresponding statistics for letters in plaintext examples of related writings. This means that monoalphabetic ciphers can never provide high-grade encryption. Of course, as we discussed in chapter 1, not all the cryptorunes are strictly monoalphabetic, so get your friends together, get some refreshments, and sharpen your pencils.

CHAPTER 3

SECRET CODES FROM THE STARS

We feel certain that the extraterrestrial message is a mathematical code of some kind. Probably a number code. Mathematics is the one language we might conceivably have in common with other forms of intelligent life in the universe. As I understand it, there is no reality more independent of our perception and more true to itself than mathematical reality.

—Don DeLillo, *Ratner's Star*

[illegible]

—Nobel laureate George Wald, Harvard University

The Codes of Flowers

What if spaceships from another world suddenly appeared in our skies? What if tomorrow morning, you turned on your radio or computer and heard a coded, pulsating tone—and learned that the same thing was happening everywhere on Earth!

For this chapter, forget about earthly secret codes and open your mind to the decryption of alien messages. Imagine that you are a computer genius watching as a teardrop-shaped spacecraft hovers above Earth and transmits a cyclic tone. The world frantically tries to understand the aliens' intentions—until you decipher the alien message. The creatures are giving earthlings one choice: become their slaves, or die. It's a countdown to weapon firing. The president of the United States tries to reason with the aliens, to no avail. They demonstrate their massive firepower by destroying New York City, and the militaries of many nations try to retaliate with little effect.

If we ever do receive a message from the stars intended to be deciphered by us, just how will it be sent, and how difficult will it be to interpret? If we decide to reply, how will we send a message? One possibility is that we (or aliens) would use radio waves beamed into space at frequencies between 1 and 10,000 megahertz, because these frequencies travel relatively easily through space and through the atmospheres of planets like our own. The first part of the message would be easy to understand, in order to attract attention. For example, it could be a series of pulses representing the numbers one, two, three, and so on. This could be followed by more intricate communications.

Could beings in other worlds already be sending out beams of electromagnetic waves modulated in some mathematical way—for example, in sequences corresponding to the prime numbers? What message would you send to the stars? In the late 1970s, Carl Sagan wanted to send music on the unmanned U.S. Voyager satellites destined to leave our solar system after exploring several planets. Sagan felt strongly that our music was a measure of our achievements and representative of our emotional and intellectual development. Other scientists wanted to send images and information on the chemistry of life on Earth. Eventually it was decided that images, natural sounds, and information could be sent on a phonograph record. But the Voyager staff wondered what sounds and images should be sent to represent a diverse sampling of life on Earth. What would you send? Here are just a few of the sounds that were finally sent into space with the Voyagers: the songs of the humpback whale, a kiss, a heartbeat, the boom of a Saturn V rocket taking off, frogs, crickets, volcanoes, laughter, and all the languages that humans speak. Images included flowers, trees, animals, oceans, deserts, supermarkets, highways, houses, and humans engaging in all sorts of activities.

Would aliens be able to decipher the images and sounds sent on the Voyager satellites? What if they misinterpreted our intent, and thought the sounds were to be interpreted as images, or the images as sounds? They'd be dancing and snapping their claws to "music" from an image of a flower. They'd "look" at the acoustical signals from the audio sections and see something quite abstract, perhaps like paintings by Willem de Kooning or Jackson Pollock.

Deciphering Coded Messages from Tiber

To a frog with its simple eye, the world is a dim array of greys and blacks. Are we like frogs in our limited sensorium, apprehending just part of the universe we inhabit? Are we as a species now awakening to the reality of multidimensional worlds in which matter undergoes subtle reorganizations in some sort of hyperspace?

—Michael Murphy, *The Future of the Body*

Many science fiction novels have dealt explicitly with alien signals and deciphering efforts. For example, in Buzz Aldrin and John Barnes's bestselling novel *Encounter with Tiber*, astronomers on Earth detect a signal from Alpha Centauri, the triple star whose faintest component is the star closest to Earth, about 4.3 light-years away.

Scientists first attempt to determine which of the stars the alien transmitter is orbiting by analyzing the Doppler effect (a shift in frequency that occurs in waves coming from a moving object).

Bits and pieces of the signal seem to be strangely ordered, like a sequence of tones, two different pitches stuttering at an enormous rate. Unfortunately, the Earth's atmosphere is nearly opaque to radio at the transmission wavelength of 96 meters, because the signal cannot easily penetrate the ionosphere. Thus, it is impossible to catch more than brief snatches of the message even with the most sensitive radio telescopes on the ground. Luckily, scientists find a way to mount simple antennas on a space station to listen to the signal.

Initially, the scientists are skeptical about the so-called signal and suspect that strange events in the Alpha Centauri stellar atmosphere are causing one star to act as a giant laser at the signal's wavelength. Perhaps a huge electrical storm in the atmosphere of a planet circling those stars could produce such a signal, and the gravity of Alpha Centauri A acts as a lens to focus and amplify radiation. The idea that the signal might be sent by aliens is discounted by many, not just because of sheer improbability but also because it seems unlikely that an intelligent species would try to contact others using radio on a wavelength that was mostly blocked by the water-vapor-rich atmosphere of a planet with life.

Although Alpha Centauri is our nearest neighbor, a spaceship would take about 110,000 years—time enough for four Ice Ages—to travel from Earth to Alpha Centauri, assuming we traveled at the speed at which the Apollo astronauts went to the moon. A radio signal, which is more than 26,500 times faster, takes about four years to traverse the distance.

Despite their skepticism, the scientists continue to study the signal, and they discover that it is a pattern of high tones, low tones, and silences. The scientists call the high tones beeps (represented below by a ...) and the low tones honks (represented by a ...). Because the transmission comes as sets of triple tones, if we assume that the silences are spaces, there are eight possible arrangements of the three tones:

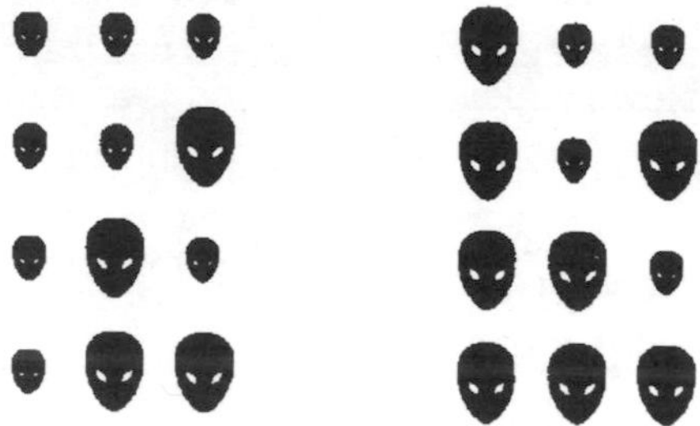

The groups of three tones are likely to stand for the digits zero through seven, which are the eight digits in a base-eight number system. The string of digits in the message could represent pictures or text.

The most common number system on Earth is base ten. In other words, we have ten digits, zero through nine. In our base-ten representation, each digit represents a power of ten. For example, the number 2,010 is $(2 \times 10^3) + (0 \times 10^2) + (1 \times 10^1) + (0 \times 10^0)$, where $10^3 = 1{,}000$, $10^2 = 100$, $10^1 = 10$, and $10^0 = 1$. However, there's no reason to assume that aliens would use a base-ten number system, and it's unlikely that a message from the stars would arrive in base-ten numbers. On Earth, our mathematical calculations are based on ten because we have ten fingers. In fact, our language suggests the connection between fingers and our number system—we use the word *digit* to designate both a number and a finger. Because our base-ten system comes from our use of ten fingers, what would a base-eight system tell us about the anatomy of aliens? Perhaps it would denote an alien with a thumb and three fingers on each hand, or a creature with eight tentacles, or one with a thumb and one finger on each of its four arms. An even wilder possibility is that the aliens have three heads and these are all the combinations of nodding and shaking that are possible! (Of course, it is possible that their number system tells us nothing about their anatomy. After all, what did the Babylonians' base-sixty system tell us about their anatomy?)

As scientists study the message, they find that it repeats every eleven hours and twenty minutes. Each group of 16,769,021 base-eight numbers takes about two and a half seconds to be received, so there are 16,384 such groups in all. What could it mean?

The first thing to check is the number 16,769,021. Does it have any unusual properties? You can use a simple factoring program to determine that it is the product of two prime numbers: 4093 x 4097. Since a prime number isn't evenly divisible by another number (except itself and one), an alien could transmit a gridlike pattern whose size is the product of two prime numbers. As a result, there are only a couple of possible arrangements for the numbers in the grid. (In fact, the pattern could be similar to a photo consisting of an array of pixels like those on your computer screen.) On the other hand, if the image were composed of, for example, 10,000,000 elements, a number with many factors, the number of possible grid arrangements would be very large—5 x 200,000, 10,000 x 1,000, and many others—and this would make the image difficult to decode.

Alien Encyclopedia

In *Encounter with Tiber*, it turns out that the eight groups of honks and beeps represent eight different intensity values in an image: zero for black, seven for white, and one through six for intermediate intensities. By representing these brightness values on a 4093 x 4097 grid, the astrophysicists determine that each transmission is a frame of a movie. When played sequentially on a computer, the frames show eight creatures waving as they climb into a spacecraft! Other more technical information follows, including instructions on how to find an alien encyclopedia containing poems, paintings, music, literature, science, engineering, and jokes of a civilization centuries in advance of Earth's.

Would you like to view such an alien encyclopedia? In *Encounter with Tiber*, some people worry that humanity is not ready for advanced knowledge from the encyclopedia. "What if you'd given Napoleon the atomic bomb?" scientists and politicians ask. "What if the Civil War had been fought with airplanes dropping poison gas on cities?" Should the encyclopedia be made available to all the nations on Earth?

Do you think that communication with aliens would create widespread hysteria? The psychologist Carl Jung believed that contact with superior beings would be devastating and demoralizing to us because we'd find we were no more a match for them intellectually than our pets are for us. Such fears and jealousies might cause various extremist groups, such as the Ku Klux Klan, to try to kill the aliens.

The Universe's Rosetta Stone

Probably the easiest method of establishing communication with an alien species is through mathematics, the universe's Rosetta stone. Any space-faring or technological race would know about mathematics. It is clear from studying our own history that mathematics has fascinated humans since the dawn of civilization. Has our long-term preoccupation with mathematics arisen because the universe is constructed from a mathematical fabric? In 1623, Galileo Galilei voiced this belief by stating his credo: "Nature's great book is written in mathematical symbols." Plato's doctrine was that God is a geometer, and Sir James Jeans believed that God experimented with arithmetic.

The fact that reality can be described or approximated by simple mathematical expressions suggests to me that nature has mathematics at its core, and technological aliens will discover the same mathematics as humans. Formulas such as $E = mc^2$, $\vec{F}=m\vec{a}$, $1+e^{i\pi}=0$, and $\lambda=h/mv$ all boggle the mind with their compactness and profundity. $E = mc^2$ is Albert Einstein's equation relating energy and mass. $\vec{F}=m\vec{a}$ is Isaac Newton's second law: force acting on a body is proportional to its mass and its acceleration. $1+e^{i\pi}=0$ is Leonhard Euler's formula relating three fundamental mathematical terms: e, π, and i. The last equation, $\lambda=h/mv$, is Louis de Broglie's wave equation indicating that matter has both wave and particle characteristics. Here the Greek letter lambda, λ, is the wavelength of the wave particle, and m is its mass.

These examples are not meant to suggest that *all* phenomena, including subatomic phenomena, are described by simple-looking formulas; however, as scientists gain more fundamental understanding, they hope to simplify many of their more unwieldy formulas. I see no reason why aliens will not discover the same truths.

God's Secret Code

Humans have thought about sending messages to the stars for decades, although there has always been some debate about what the message should contain. For example, in the 1970s, Soviet researchers suggested we send the message:

$$10^2 + 11^2 + 12^2 = 13^2 + 14^2$$

The Soviets called the equation "mind-catching."

They pointed out that the sums on each side of the equal sign total 365—the number of days in an Earth year. These imaginative Soviets went further to say that extraterrestrials had actually adjusted the Earth's rotation to bring about this striking equality! Surely it would catch aliens' attention and demonstrate our mathematical prowess.

I find the Soviet formula arbitrary and not a good candidate to send. Rather, I would somehow try to send the most profound and enigmatic formula known to humans:

$$1+e^{i\pi}=0$$

Some believe that this compact formula is surely proof of a Creator. Others have actually called $1+e^{i\pi}=0$ "God's formula." Edward Kasner and James Newman, in *Mathematics and the Imagination,* note, "We can only reproduce the equation and not stop to inquire into its implications. It appeals equally to the mystic, the scientist, the mathematician." Created by Leonhard Euler (1707–1783), the formula unites the five most important symbols of mathematics: 1, 0, π, e, and *i* (the square root of minus one). This union was regarded as a mystic union containing representatives from each branch of the mathematical tree: Arithmetic is represented by 0 and 1, algebra by the symbol *i*, geometry by π, and analysis by the transcendental number e. Harvard mathematician Benjamin Pierce said about the formula, "That is surely true, it is absolutely paradoxical; we cannot understand it, and we don't know what it means, but we have proved it, and therefore we know it must be the truth."

Another beautiful and wondrous expression involves a limit that connects not only π and e but also radicals, factorials, and infinite limits. Surely this little-known beauty makes the gods weep for joy:

$$\lim_{n \to \infty} \frac{e^n n!}{n^n \cdot \sqrt{n}} = \sqrt{2\pi}$$

There is just one problem in sending either of these two formulas to the stars. Numbers like π (3.1415 . . .) and e (2.7182 . . .) contain an infinite number of digits, so we'd have to think of compact ways to represent them. For example, π could be represented diagrammatically by indicating the ratio of a circle's circumference to its diameter. The number e might be represented by an exponential growth curve. However, despite the elegance and profundity of this formula, I admit that it is more straightforward to send pulses corresponding to integers such as prime numbers, which would easily serve to focus aliens' attention on the signal. Occasionally, we, or the aliens, can intersperse instructions on how to build better receivers, transmitters, and so forth.

Whatever the attention-getting signal is, it should be simple. For example, if aliens started with attention-getting signals that were too complex, their attempt would be like trying to make first contact with a prehistoric jungle tribe using a Pentium computer instead of banging on a piece of wood. More sophisticated communication can come later.

The Code Breakers

[illegible]

Imagine how difficult it could be to decipher an alien language. Recall how much difficulty anthropologists and linguists had in deciphering lost languages on our own planet. If Napoleon's troops had not discovered the Rosetta stone near the mouth of the Nile, Jean Champollion could not have deciphered the hieroglyphics of ancient Egypt. We still can't decipher the Etruscan language spoken by the ancient people of Etruria in Italy, who were early neighbors of the Romans. Etruscan does not seem to be an Indo-European language, and it is known mostly from thousands of short, repetitious inscriptions and an ancient text of 281 lines written on strips of linen cloth. These strips were originally part of a book that was later cut into strips and used in Egypt as a wrapping for a mummy. Another clue comes from a bronze model of a sheep's liver found at Piacenza, which has only forty-five words on it.

Despite many attempts to decipher them and some claims of success, the Etruscan records still defy translation. For some words the grammatical category has been established, and for a smaller number a meaning has been assigned.

Even knowing that Etruscan writing has an alphabet derived from one of the Greek alphabets, and therefore that sound values can be assigned to each symbol, we still can't do much translating. If we can't translate Etruscan, could we hope to decipher a message from Alpha Centauri?

We have another fascinating example of how difficult it might be to understand an alien message. The mysterious Voynich manuscript here on Earth has defied all attempts to ferret out its meaning. Dating at least to 1586, the manuscript was written in a language of which no other example is known to exist. Its alphabetic script consists of between nineteen and twenty-eight letters, none of which resemble any English or European letters. The manuscript is more than a hundred pages long, written in free running hand, an example of which is:

Of course there would be one major difference between either the Etruscan or the Voynich language and alien messages beamed to us from outer space. Can you figure out what it is?

Aliens hoping for contact would try to make their messages as easy to understand as possible. They would be practicing anticryptography, the science of designing codes as easy as possible to decipher. Because technological beings will understand not only mathematics but also the structures of various atoms and molecules, the positions of stars, and the physics of relativity, these kinds of information may establish a common starting language.

Some astronomers and mathematicians believe that symbolic logic is the best way for intelligent beings from different star systems to communicate. In the 1960s, Hans Freudenthal, professor of mathematics at the University of Utrecht in the Netherlands, attempted to develop a logical language that we could use to communi-

Ha Inq *Ha*:
x ∈ Hom.→:Ini.*x*Ext·—:Ini·Cor*x*.Ext˙=
Cca.Sec 11 × 10^10111:
∨*x*˙*x* ∈ Bes.∧:Ini.*x*Ext·—:Ini·Cor*x*.Ext˙>Sec 0:
x ∈ Hom.→˙∨ ⌈*y*.*z*⌉:*y* ⌢ *z* ∈ Hom.∧·*y* = .Mat *x*·∧·*z* =.Pat*x*:
∨*x*:*x* ∈ Bes.∧˙∨ ⌈*y*.*z*⌉:*y* ⌢ *z* ∈ Bes.∧·*y* = .Mat *x*·∧·*z* =.Pat*x*:
x ∈ Hom.→:∧*t*:Ini·Cor*x*.Ext:Ant:*t*.Ant:Ini.*x* Ext˙
→:*t* Cor*x*.Par·*t* Cor.Mat *x*:
∨*x*:*x* ∈ Bes.∧·∧*t*.Etc:
x ∈ Hom.∧:*s* = Ini·Cor *x*.Ext·
→:∨ ⌈*u*.*v*⌉*s* Cor*u*.Par·*s* Cor.Mat*x*:
∧˙PauAnt.*s*·Cor *v*.Par:PauAnt.*s*·Cor.Pat*x*˙
∧:*s* Cor *x*.Uni·*s* Cor*u*.*s* Cor*v*:
∨*x*:*x* ∈ Bes.∧.Etc:
Hom=Hom Fem.∪.Hom Msc:
Hom Fem∩Hom Msc=⌈ ⌉:
Car:⌉*x*·Nnc*x*Ext.∧.*x* ∈ Hom Fem˙
Pau>˙Car:⌉*x*·Nnc*x*Ext.∧.*x* ∈ Hom Msc:
y = Mat*x*.∧.*y* ∈ Hom·→.*y* ∈ Hom Fem:∧:
y = Pat*x*.∧.*y* ∈ Hom·→.*y* ∈ Hom Msc:
x ∈ Hom∪Bes:→:Fin.Cor*x*·Pst.Fin*x*#

fig. 9

cate with intelligent aliens with whom we have nothing in common. The language is called *Lincos*, which stands for Lingua Cosmica, and it consists of mathematical, biological, and linguistic symbols, including some used by earlier mathematical logicians such as Alfred North Whitehead and Bertrand Russell. In Lincos, the lexicon and syntax are built up gradually, starting with elementary arithmetical concepts and advancing to more complex abstract ideas. Can you decode any of the message in figure 9 written in the language of Lincos? A bit of explanation regarding Lincos is provided in chapter 7, "Solutions."

How would you code a message to be interpreted by extraterrestrials? What information would you send? Should humans be sending messages to the stars? Do you think a majority of the people on Earth would be happy to receive an intelligent signal from an advanced extraterrestrial civilization? What effect would this have on politics, religion, and philosophy?

Even if aliens made prodigious attempts to make their messages understandable, how much could we understand from very different creatures transmitting at very long or rapid timescales—for example a technological species inhabiting the surface of a neutron star, living out their lives in a fraction of a second, as in Robert L. Forward's *Dragon's Egg*. What could we have to say to creatures with whom we have so little in common? As author John Casti notes in *Paradigms Lost*, perhaps alien science would be no more comprehensible to us than the wiring diagram of an IBM PC is to a member of a nonliterate aboriginal tribe. If aliens send political, cultural, and ethical information, the signal may suggest practices or systems that we would find immoral or just plain unworkable, for example, the cannibalization of children, the abolition of money, the practice of sex with plants, or the rationing of love. This alienness has led John Casti to suggest that the benefits from the SETI (Search for Extraterrestrial Intelligence) project are overestimated. Casti believes that, even if extraterrestrial intelligences exist, we'll never know them or get any real benefit from them, simply because they are truly and fundamentally alien. I take an opposite view and believe that the mere act of searching is important. Searching and wondering are what science is all about. As Richard Powers noted in *The Gold Bug Variations*, "Science is not about control. It is about cultivating a perpetual condition of wonder in the face of something that forever grows one step richer and subtler than our latest theory about it. It is about reverence, not mastery."

Chapter 4

The Cryptorunes

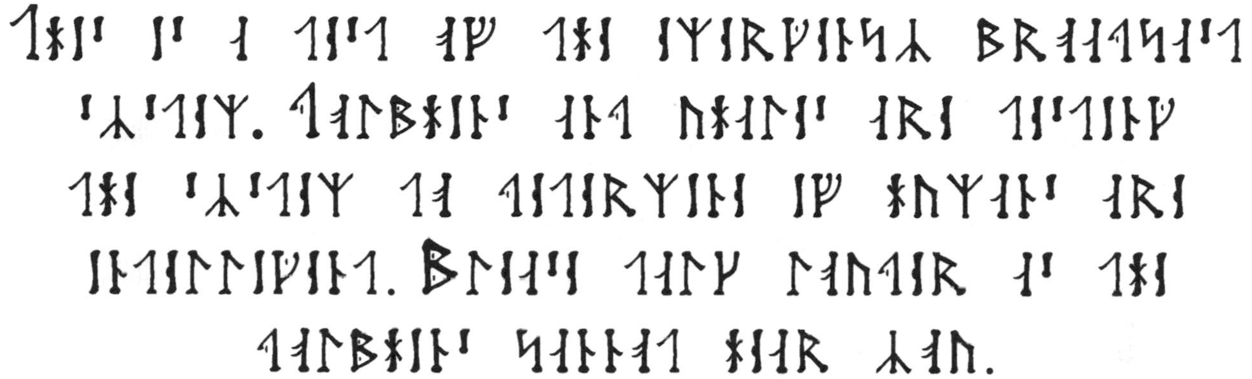

[runic text]

Are you ready for an intriguing adventure? As I've discussed, many cryptorunes are not ordinary monoalphabetic substitution codes. To make them just a bit more challenging, in a few instances, one English letter is represented by the same two adjacent runes (a double-rune). In a few other instances, a single rune represents two or three different English letters. The mapping of letters to runes changes from one cryptorune to the next. Here are some hints to bring some sanity into the life of a budding cryptoruneologist:

- The double-runes [rune][rune], [rune][rune], and [rune][rune] can stand for a single English letter.
- The runes [rune], [rune], [rune], and [rune] can stand for two different English letters.
- The symbol [rune] can stand for three different English letters.
- Dancing men with a flag, such as [dancing man], denote letters at the ends of words.

I wish you a safe journey. If you get stuck, skip to the next problem or see chapter **6**, which provides a hint for each cryptorune puzzle.

1. Can We Ever Comprehend Our Vast Cosmos?

Hints: one of the letters in the English language is represented by the two adjacent symbols [illegible]. The symbol [illegible] is used to represent two different English letters.

2. How Should We Live?

Hints: The rune [illegible] stands for two different English letters. The symbol [illegible] stands for three different English letters. The pair of symbols [illegible] stands for one English letter.

3. Do We Make Progress?

Hints: The symbol ᛚ stands for two different letters. The symbol ᛉ also stands for two different letters.

[illegible]

[illegible]

[illegible]

—[illegible] ([illegible])

4. The Devil?

Hint: The double-rune ᚹᛣ stands for a single English letter.

[illegible]

[illegible]

[illegible]

[illegible]

[illegible]

[illegible]

—[illegible]

5. Motion

This quotation is from one of the most controversial figures of twentieth-century psychology and philosophy. His writings—a captivating mix of psychoanalysis, mysticism, existentialism, and left-wing politics—make for powerful and often disturbing reading.

6. Where Are You?

In 1945, an Egyptian farmer named Muhammed 'Ali uncovered a small clay jar in some cliffs near Nag Hammadi on the Nile. The jar contained thirteen codices full of ancient Coptic writings on Jesus. Coptic is an Egyptian language in use during the time of Christian missionary efforts in the second century A.D.

Hint: The symbols used in this puzzle are the dancing men figures used in Arthur Conan Doyle's famous 1903 Sherlock Holmes story "The Dancing Men." The flags indicate letters at the end of words. The mapping from English letters to dancing men is not the same one used by Conan Doyle.

7. God and Technology

8. Passing On

Hints: The rune ᛇ can stand for two different English letters. The symbol ᚢ can stand for three different English letters. The pair of symbols ᚹᚢ stands for one English letter.

9. The Mystery of Space

The creator of the complete theoretical formulation of quantum mechanics is mysterious and poetic in this cryptorune.

Hints: The rune ᛁ stands for two different English letters. The symbol ᚢ stands for three different English letters. The pair of symbols ᚹᚢ stands for one English letter.

ᚽ ᚢᛏᚽᛒᛂ ᛚᛯ ᛌᚹᚢᚢᛚᛌᛘ: ᛌᚹᚢ ᛂᚹᚢᛂᛌ ᛯᚢᚽᛒᛂ, ᛉᛌᛏᛂᛯᛯ ᚽᚢ

ᛚᚢᛯ ᚢᛂᚽᛁᚢ, ᚽ ᛁᛚᚹᛉᛁᛂ ᛯᚢᚽᛌᛋᛯ.

—ᚢᚽᛉᛏ ᛋᛚᛁᚽᛒ

10. What Is Love?

This quotation is from the Bishop of Hippo (in Roman Africa) from A.D. 396 to 430.

ᛈᛣᚷᚺ ᚼᚱᛗᛁ ᛒᛉᛚᚺ—ᛉᚳᛝ ᛗᛁᚺᚳ ᚼᛁᛉᛗ ᛋᛣᚳ ᚼᚱᛈᛈ, ᛝᛣ.

—ᚠᛗ. ᛉᚳᛏᚳᚠᛗᚱᛣᚺ

11. From the Psalms

ᛁᚠ ᛁᚦ ᚳᛣᛘ ᚠᚠᛟᚠ ᚳᛁᛋᛘᛚᚠᚠ ᛩᛚ ᚹᛁᚠᚠ ᚦᚠᛋᛚᚺᚳᚠᚠ....

ᚠᛚ ᚠᛚᛟᛚᚠᛚᚠᚠ ᛩᛏ ᚠᛟᚺᛘᚦ ᚠᛣ ᚹᛟᛋ.

—ᛣᚦᛟᛒᛩ 18:32, 34

12. On the Nature of Reality

Seth is the acclaimed nonphysical teacher who spoke through a prolific author while she was in a trance.

ᛀᚪᛕ ᚠᚦᚹ ᚴᚪ ᛯᚠᚦᚱ ᚪᛏ ᚱᛃᚹ ᚼᚪᚦᛉ ᚱᛃᚠᚱ ᛀᚪᛕᚦ

ᚴᛉᛉᛃᛃᚱᚹᚴᚱ ᚠᚠᚱᛉᚪᛏ ᚠᚪᛏᚱᚦᛉᛦᛕᚱᚹᚴ ᚱᚪ ᛉᚱᚴ ᚦᚹᚴᛉᛉᚱᛀ.

ᛀᚪᛕᚦ ᛦᚦᚹᚠᚱᛃ ᚠᛃᚠᛏᛃᚹᚴ ᚱᛃᚹ ᚠᚱᚼᚪᚴᛯᛃᚹᚦᚹ. ᛀᚪᛕᚦ

ᚹᛏᚠᚪᛕᛏᚱᚹᚦᚴ ᚼᛉᚱᛃ ᚪᚱᛃᚹᚦᚴ ᚠᛉᚱᚹᚦ ᚱᛃᚹ ᛏᚠᛦᚦᛉᚠᚴ ᚪᛏ

ᚱᛃᚹᛉᚦ ᛉᛉᛒᚹᚴ, ᚠᛏ ᚱᛃᚹ ᛉᛉᛒᚹᚴ ᚪᛏ ᚱᛃᚪᚴᚹ ᚼᛃᚪ ᚠᚪᚼᚹ

ᛉᛏ ᚠᚪᛏᚱᚠᚠᚱ ᚼᛉᚱᛃ ᚱᛃᚹᚼ.

—ᚢᚠᛏᚹ ᚦᚪᛦᚹᚦᚱᚴ

13. On the Danger of Dreams

ᛒᚼᛉ ᛗᛋᚠᚻ ᛦᛋᛚᛞ ᚳᛗᛋᚳ ᚳᛗᚻ ᚹᛋᚢᛞ ᛚᛦ ᛋ ᛞᚹᚻᛋᚻ

ᛦᚼᚹ ᛒᚼᛉ—ᛋᚢᛞ ᚳᛗᛋᚳ ᛒᚼᛉ ᛦᚻᛋᚹ ᚳᚼ ᛁᚻ ᚻᛋᛞᚻ ᚻᛋᛞ.

ᛁᛉᚳ ᚻᛋᛞᚢᚻᛦᛦ ᛚᛦ ᚢᚼᚳ ᚳᛗᚻ ᚼᚢᚹᛒ ᛞᛋᚢᚣᚻᚹ ᛚᚢ

ᛞᚹᚻᛋᚻᛦ. ᚳᛗᚻᚹᚻ ᛚᛦ ᛋᚹᛦᚼ ᚳᛗᚻ ᛞᛋᚢᚣᚻᚹ ᚳᛗᛋᚳ

ᛦᚼᚻᚻᚳᛗᛚᚢᚣ ᚻᛋᛒ ᛁᚻ ᚹᚼᛦᚳ ᛦᚹᛗᛚᚷᛗ ᚷᛋᚢ ᚢᚻᚠᚻᚹ ᛁᚻ

ᚹᚻᚣᛋᛚᚢᚻᛞ.

—ᛦ. ᚹ. ᛞᚼᚢᛋᚹᛞᛦᚼᚢ, ᚹᚼᚹᛞ ᛦᚼᛉᚹ'ᛦ ᛁᛋᚢᚻ

14. Do Not Cry

ᛕᚦ ᛦᚴᚾᛩᛩ, ᚺᚦᛣᛰᚴ: ᐳᛣᛒᚦ ᛃᛘ ᚦᛟᛁᛘᛦᚴᚴᛣᛩᛣᚴᚾᛘᛃ. ᚺᛘᛩᚨ
ᛁᚦᛣᚹᚦ ᛣᛃᚨ ᛋᛰᚾᚦᚴ, ᛣᛃᚨ ᛕᚦ ᛦᚴᚾᛩᛩ.
—ᛦ. ᛰ. ᚨᛘᛃᛣᛩᚨᛦᛘᛃ, ᛩᛘᛰᚨ ᚴᛘᚴᛣᛩ'ᛦ ᛕᛣᛃᚦ

15. Dreaming

The following cryptorune is from a Lebanese-American philosophical essayist, novelist, mystical poet, and artist. His works were especially influential in American popular culture in the 1960s.

ᚺX ᚺXᚹᛦ ᚢXᚹᚢᚳ, ᛒXᚢ ᚺX ᛁᛏᚠᚤ ᚺᛏᛦ ᛋᛁᚹᛗᚱXᛦ
ᚹᚠᚢ ᚱXᚹᚹᚢᛞᚺᚹᛁ ᚢᛦXᚹᛗᛋ.
—ᚨᚹᚳᛁᛞᛁ ᚤᛞᚱᛦᚹᚠ

16. A Dark Pit

ᛦᛗᛈ ᚷᛗᛋᛘᚺ ᛘᛋᛘ ᚺᛈᚹᛈᚹᛒ ᚾᚢᛈ ᚾᚳ ᛦᛗᛈ ᚾᚹᛚᚳᛚᚷᛈᛘ ᚾᚳ
ᛦᛗᛋᛦ ᛁᛚᛦ ᚾᚳ ᚾᚹᛋᚷᛗᚢᛈᛘᛘ ᛦᛗᛋᛦ ᚹᛚᛈᛘ ᚾᛈᚢᛈᛋᛦᛗ ᛘᛘ,
ᛈᚠᛈᚹᛒᛏᛗᛈᚹᛈ.
—ᛘ. ᚠ. ᛗᚾᚢᛋᚹᛗᛘᚾᚳ, ᚹᚾᚹᛗ ᚳᚾᛘᚹ'ᛘ ᚾᛋᚢᛈ

17. Men and Women

The German-born Swiss novelist and poet quoted in this cryptorune won the Nobel Prize for literature in 1946. The theme of many of his novels was the conflicts experienced by young people—especially creative artists—in search of self.

18. Peace

The author of this quotation, a German poet, dramatist, novelist, and scientist, created poetry that expressed a modern view of humanity's relationship to nature, history, and society. His plays and novels reflect a profound understanding of human individuality.

19. Power

The 700-verse Sanskrit poem from which this is taken is regarded by most Hindus as their most important text—the essence of their belief. Almost every significant Hindu philosopher has written a commentary on this work, and new translations and interpretations continue to appear.

20. Peter Pan

This statement is from a Scottish journalist, playwright, and children's-book writer who lived from 1860 to 1937.

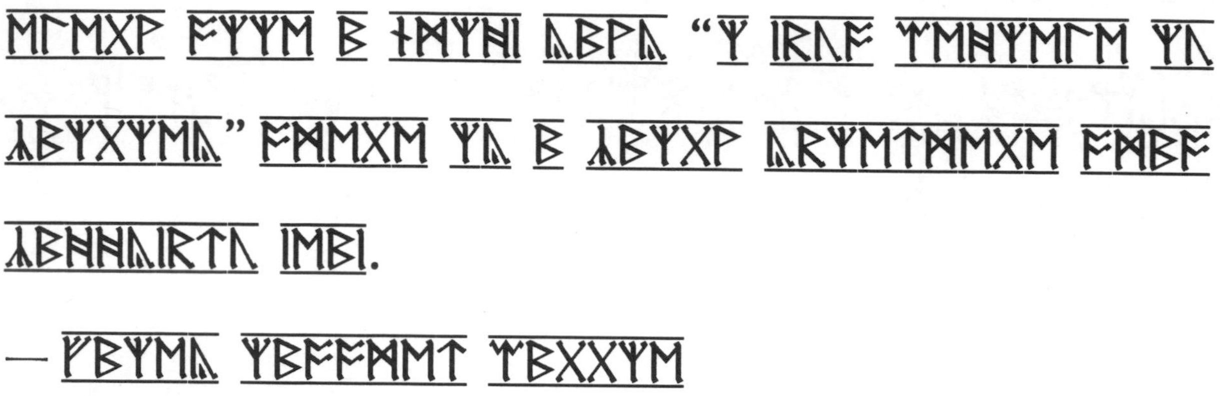

21. In a Forest

The author of this quotation was born in 1926 in Leigh-on-Sea, a small town about forty miles from London in the county of Essex. The mysterious book from which this was taken has developed a cult following in the United States.

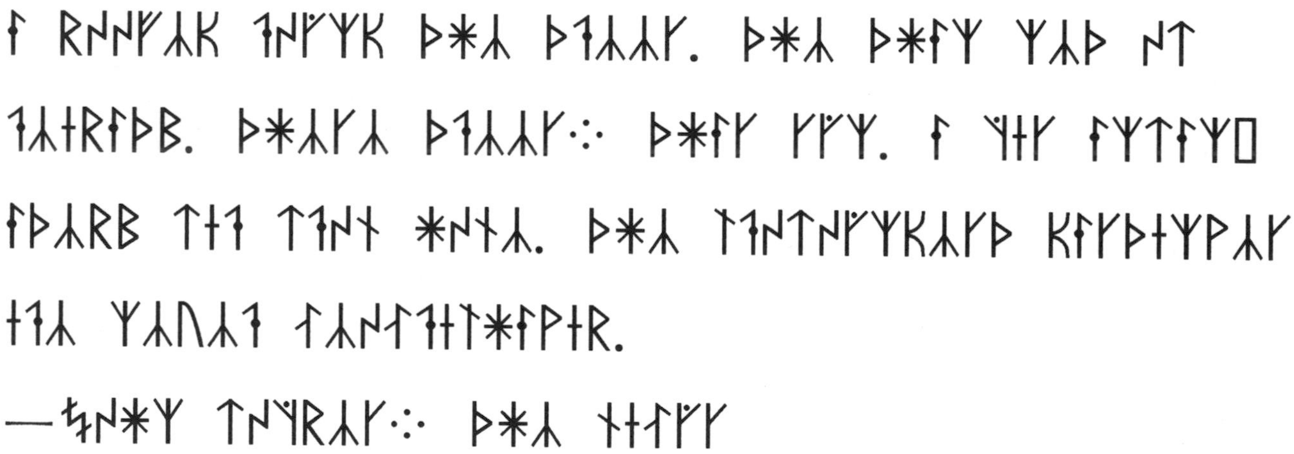

22. Ghosts

The Norwegian dramatist quoted here wrote well-constructed plays dealing realistically with psychological and social problems. He is recognized as the father of modern drama.

ᛦ ᚱᚠᛦ ᛒᚱᚲᚠ ᛦᛋᛘᚲᛦᛋᚺᛁ ᚢᛏ ᚢᛒᛦᛋᚦ ᚴᚺ ᚱᚹᚺ ᚱᚲᚲ ᚠᛒᛏᛋᚢᛋ.... ᚢᛒᚺᛟ ᚱᚹᚺ ᛋᛏᚢ ᚱᛘᚢᚴᚱᚲᚲᛟ ᚱᚲᛦᚼᚺ ᛦᛋ ᚴᛋ; ᚴᚴᚢ ᚢᛒᚺᚹᚺ ᚢᛒᚺᛟ ᚱᚹᚺ ᛁᛏᚹᚠᚱᛋᚢ, ᚱᚲᚲ ᚢᛒᚺ ᛋᚱᚠᛦᚺ, ᚱᛋᛁ ᚴᚺ ᛘᚱᛋ ᛋᚺᚼᚺᚹ ᚴᚺ ᚹᛦᛁ ᛏᚠ ᚢᛒᚺᚠᛦ. ᚴᛒᚺᛋᚺᚼᚺᚹ ᛦ ᚢᚱᚦᚺ ᚴᚨ ᚱ ᛋᚺᚴᛋᚨᚱᚨᚺᚹ ᚱᛋᛁ ᚹᚺᚱᛁ ᛦᚢ, ᛦ ᚠᚱᛋᛘᛟ ᛦ ᛋᚺᚺ ᚠᛒᛏᛋᚢᛋ ᛘᚹᚺᚺᚨᛦᛋᚠ ᚴᚺᚢᚴᚺᚺᛋ ᚢᛒᚺ ᚲᛦᛋᚺᛋ. ᚢᛒᚺᚹᚺ ᚠᛦᚴᛋᚢ ᚴᚺ ᚠᛒᛏᛋᚢᛋ ᚱᚲᚲ ᛏᚼᚺᚹ ᚢᛒᚺ ᚴᛏᚹᚲᛁ. ᚢᛒᚺᛟ ᚠᛦᚴᛋᚢ ᚴᚺ ᚱᛋ ᛘᛏᚴᛋᚢᚲᚺᛋᛋ ᚱᛋ ᚠᚹᚱᛦᛋᛋ ᛏᚠ ᛋᚱᛋᛁ ᛦᚢ ᛋᚺᚺᚠᛦᛋ ᚢᛏ ᚠᛦᚺ. ᚱᛋᛁ ᚴᚺ ᚱᚹᚺ ᛋᛏ ᚠᛦᛦᛋᚺᚹᚱᚴᚲᛟ ᚱᚠᚹᚱᛦᛁ ᛏᚠ ᚢᛒᚺ ᚲᛦᚠᛒᚢ, ᚱᚲᚲ ᛏᚠ ᚴᛋ.

—ᛒᚺᛋᚹᛦᚦ ᛦᚴᛋᚺᛋ

23. Poetry

ᛉᚺᛞᚺᛞ ᛗᚺᛞ ᛉᛚᚼᛞᛦ ᚼᚺᛞᛗ ᛦᛚᚱᛞᛗᚹᛞ ᛚᛦ ᛗ ᛁᚳᛞᚼ.

—ᛘᚳᚺᛗ ᛏᚳᚼᚱᛞᛦ, ᛉᚺᛞ ᚼᛗᛘᚷᛦ

24. Can You Sing Softly?

Some say that the brujo shaman of Los Angeles who wrote this passage gave dignity to the common people of Mexico with his revolutionary books about Don Juan, a simple healer in the desert, who caught the imagination of the world.

ᚠᛗᛖ ᛡᚱᚢᛁᛦᚠᛦᚱᚢᚥ ᚱᚳ ᛒ ᚥᚱᚺᛦᚠᛒᚷᚹ ᚴᚹᛦᚷᛁ ᛒᚷᛖ ᚳᛦᛚᛖ: ᚳᛦᚷᚥᚠ, ᚠᛗᛒᚠ ᛦᚠ ᚳᚺᛦᛖᚥ ᚠᚱ ᚠᛗᛖ ᛗᛦᚴᛗᛖᚥᚠ ᛞᚱᛦᚢᚠ. ᚥᛖᛡᚱᚢᛁ, ᚠᛗᛒᚠ ᛦᚠ ᛁᚱᛖᚥ ᚢᚱᚠ ᚥᛁᚳᚳᛖᚷ ᚳᚱᚷ ᛡᚱᛉᛞᛒᚢᚹ, ᚢᚱᚠ ᛖᛚᛖᚢ ᚱᚳ ᛦᚠᚥ ᚱᛏᚢ ᚺᛦᚢᛁ. ᚠᛗᛦᚷᛁ, ᚠᛗᛒᚠ ᛦᚠ ᛒᛦᛉᚥ ᛦᚠᚥ ᚴᚹᛖᛒᚺ ᚠᚱ ᚠᛗᛖ ᚥᚺᚹ. ᚳᚱᛁᚷᚠᛗ, ᚠᛗᛒᚠ ᛦᚠ ᛁᚱᛖᚥ ᚢᚱᚠ ᛗᛒᛚᛖ ᛒ ᛁᛖᚳᛦᚢᛦᚠᛖ ᛡᚱᚺᚱᚷ. ᚳᛦᚳᚠᛗ, ᚠᛗᛒᚠ ᛦᚠ ᚥᛦᚢᚴᚥ ᛚᛖᚷᚹ ᚥᚱᚳᚠᚺᚹ.

—ᛡᛒᚷᚺᚱᚥ ᛡᛒᚥᚠᛒᚢᛖᛁᛒ, ᚠᛒᚺᛖᚥ ᚱᚳ ᛞᚱᛏᛖᚷ

25. Rebirth

The author of this statement is a Mexican novelist, short story writer, playwright, critic, and diplomat who published experimental novels that won him an international literary reputation.

ᛈᛚᛈ ᛁᚥ ᚹᚴᛡᚥ ᚺᚥᛞᚥ ᛉᚴ ᚱᛖᚷᛦᚺ ᚴᛞ ᚹᛞᛒ? ᛖᛞᚥ ᛁᚥ ᛈᛒᛚᛗᛦ ᚴᛞ ᚢᚥᛚᛗᛦ ᚢᚴᛞᛗ?

—ᚹᛖᛞᚱᚴᚳ ᛏᚷᚥᛗᛉᚥᚳ, ᛉᚥᛞᛞᛖ ᛗᚴᚳᛉᛞᛖ

26. The Oneness of Nature

With doctorates in anthropology and ethology and additional degrees in botany, chemistry, geology, geography, marine biology, and ecology, the author of this cryptorune speculates on whimsical and unusual events, searching for beautiful images whether natural or manufactured.

✱ᛐᚴᚽ ᛦᛘᚠᛐᛐᛐᚽᛦ ᛐᚠ ᛋᛉᚽ ᚽᛉᛒᚱᛦ ᚱᚴ ᛋᛉᚽ ᚽᚱᛦᛋᚱᛦ ᚦᚹ

ᛐᛐᚽᛕᛐᚠᚿ ᚱᚠᛏᚽᚠ ᚱᛘᛋ ᚱᚴ ᛋᛉᚽ ᛏᛐᚠᛏᛦ. ᛏᚽᛒᛋᛉ ᛐᛦ ᚽᚽᚠᛋᛒᛐᚠ∴

ᚦᛘᛋ ✱ᛐᚴᚽ ᚦᚽᚽᚱᛋᚽᛦ ᛐᚱᛦᛦᛐᚦ✱ᚽ ᚦᚹ ᚴᚱ✱✱ᚱᛏᛐᚠᚿ ᛐᛒᛋᛋᚽᚠᚠᛦ

ᛋᛉᛒᛋ ✱ᚽᛒᛏ ✱ᛐᛕᚽ ᛐᛒᛋᛉᛦ ᚱᚴ ᚴᛐᚠᛋᚽᚠ ᚿᚠᚱᛘᚠᛏ ᛋᛉᚴᚱᛘᚿᛉ

ᛋᛉᚽ ᛦᛐᛒᛋᛐᛦ ᚱᚴ ᛋᛐᛋᚽ. ᚽᚹᚽ✱ᚽᛦ ᚱᚴ ✱ᛐᚿᛉᛋ ᛒᚠᛏ ᛏᛒᚴᛕ∴

ᚱᚴ ᛉᚽᛒᛋ ᛒᚠᛏ ᚽᚱ✱ᛏ∴ ᚱᚴ ᛋᛒᚿᚠᚽᛋᛐᛦᛋ∴ ᚴᛒᛏᛐᚱᛒᚽᛋᛐᚽᛐᛋᚹ∴

ᛒᚠᛏ ᚿᚠᛒᚽᛐᛋᚹ ᛒ✱✱ ᛐᚠᚱᚽᛐᛏᚽ ᚽᛐᛋᛒ✱ ᚿᛘᛐᛏᛦ—ᛒᚠᛏ ✱ᛐᚴᚽ

✱ᚽᛒᚴᚠᛦ ᛋᚱ ᚴᚽᛦᛐᚱᚠᛏ ᛋᚱ ᚽᚽᚽᚠ ᛋᛉᚽᛐᚠ ᛋᚱᛦᛋ ᛦᛘᚦᛋ✱ᚽ ᛦᛐᚿᚠᛦ.

ᛋᛉᚽ ᚽᛋᚽᚠᚿᚽᚠᚽᚽ ᚱᚴ ᛒ ᚴᚠᛘᛐᛋᚠ✱ᚹ ᛐᛦ ᛋᛘᚠᚽᛐ ᚦᚹ ᛒ ᛦᛐᛒᚴᛕ

✱ᛒᛦᛋᛐᚠᚿ ᚱᚠᚽ ᛋᛉᚱᛘᛦᛒᚠᛏᛋᛉ ᚱᚴ ᛒ ᛦᚽᚽᚱᚠᛏ; ᛋᛉᚽ ᚦᚠᚽᚽᛏᛐᚠᚿ

ᚱᚴ ᛒ ᚦᚠᛐᛦᛋ✱ᚽᛏᚱᚠᛋ ᛐᛦ ᚽᚱᚱᚠᛏᛐᚠᛒᛋᚽᛏ ᚱᚠ ᛋᛉᚽ ᚱᚽᚽᛒᚠ

ᚴ✱ᚱᚱᚠ ᚦᚹ ᛒ ᚿ✱ᛐᛋᛋᚽᚠ ᚱᚴ ✱ᛐᚿᛉᛋ ᚴᚽᚠ✱ᚽᛋᚽᛏ ᚴᚠᚱᛋ ᛋᛉᚽ

ᛋᚱᚱᚠ.... ᚠᚱᛋᛉᛐᚠᚿ ᛉᛒᛐᛐᚽᚠᛦ ᛐᚠ ᛐᛦᚱ✱ᛒᛋᛐᚱᚠ. ᛏᚽ ᚦᚠᚽᛒᛋᛉᚽ

ᛒᚠᛏ ᚦ✱ᚽᚽᛏ∴ ᛏᚽ ✱ᛒᛘᚿᛉ ᛒᚠᛏ ᚽᚠᚹ∴ ᛏᚽ ᚽᚠᛒᛦᛉ ᛒᚠᛏ ᛏᛐᚽ ᛐᚠ

ᛋᛐᛋᚽ ᛏᛐᛋᛉ ᚽᚱᛦᛋᛐᚽ ᚽᛘᚽᛦ.

—✱ᚹᛒ✱✱ ᛏᛒᛋᛦᚱᚠ∴ ᛦᛘᚽᚠᚠᛒᛋᛘᚴᚽ

27. Nearby Worlds

The American philosopher and psychologist (1842–1910) quoted here developed the philosophy of pragmatism.

ᚱᚼᚷ ᚢᚱᚷᛉᛒᚻ ᛏᛒᛈᛉᚢᚳ ᚾᚱᚢᚣᚾᛉᚱᚼᚣᚢᛗᚣᚣ ᛉᚣ ᛉᚼᚠ ᚱᚢᛗ
ᚣᚻᛗᚾᛉᛒᚻ ᚠᚦᚻᛗ ᚱᛦ ᚾᚱᚢᚣᚾᛉᚱᚼᚣᚢᛗᚣᚣ, ᛏᚻᛉᚻᚣᚠ ᛒᚻᚻ
ᛒᛉᚱᚼᚠ ᛉᚠ, ᚻᛒᚷᚠᛗᛁ ᛦᚷᚱᛉ ᛉᚠ ᛉᚦ ᚠᚻᛗ ᛦᛉᚻᛉᛉᛗᚣᚠ
ᚱᛦ ᚣᚾᚷᛗᛗᚢᚣ, ᚠᚻᛗᚷᛗ ᚻᛉᛗ ᚻᚱᚠᛗᚢᚠᛉᛒᚻ ᛦᚱᚷᛉᚣ ᚱᛦ
ᚾᚱᚢᚣᚾᛉᚱᚼᚣᚢᛗᚣᚣ ᛗᚢᚠᛉᚷᛗᚻᚦ ᛁᛉᛦᛦᛗᚷᛗᚢᚠ ᚢᚱ ᛒᚾᚾᚱᚼᚢᚠ
ᚱᛦ ᚠᚻᛗ ᚼᚢᛉᛚᛗᚷᚣᛗ ᛉᚢ ᛉᚠᚣ ᚠᚱᚠᛒᚻᛉᚠᚦ ᚾᛒᚢ ᛉᛗ
ᛦᛉᚢᛒᚻ ᛏᚻᛉᚾᚻ ᚻᛗᛒᛚᛗᚣ ᚠᚻᛗᚣᛗ ᚱᚠᚻᛗᚷ ᛦᚱᚷᛉᚣ ᚱᛦ
ᚾᚱᚢᚣᚾᛉᚱᚼᚣᚢᛗᚣᚣ ᚢᚼᛉᚠᛗ ᛁᛉᚣᚷᛗᚳᛒᚷᛁᛗᛁ ᚠᚻᛗᚦ ᛉᛒᚦ
ᛁᛗᚠᛗᚷᛉᛉᛉᚢᛗ ᛒᚠᚠᛉᚠᚼᛁᛗᚣ ᚠᚻᚱᚼᚳᚻ ᚠᚻᛗᚦ ᚾᛒᚢᚢᚱᚠ
ᛦᚼᚷᚢᛉᚣᚻ ᛦᚱᚷᛉᚼᚻᛒᚣ, ᛒᚢᛁ ᚱᚻᛗᚢ ᛒ ᚷᛗᚳᛉᚱᚢ ᚠᚻᚱᚼᚳᚻ
ᚠᚻᛗᚦ ᛦᛒᛉᚻ ᚠᚱ ᚳᛉᛚᛗ ᛒ ᛉᛒᚻ

—ᛏᛉᚻᚻᛉᛒᛉ ᚹᛒᛉᛗᚣ, ᚠᚻᛗ ᛚᛒᚷᛉᛗᚠᛉᛗᚣ ᚱᛦ ᚷᛗᚻᛉᚳᛉᚱᚼᚣ
ᛗᛋᚻᛗᚷᛉᛗᚢᚾᛗ

28. Warriors

This quotation is from one of the most powerful and complex fantasy trilogies since *Lord of the Rings.*

29. Birth

30. What Is Fear?

The quotation that follows is by an American-born English poet, literary critic, dramatist, and winner of the Nobel Prize for literature who lived from 1888 to 1965 and whose poems are among the most widely discussed literary works of the early twentieth century.

31. The Edge of Humanity

32. Unhappiness

33. Togetherness

This quotation is by a German-born U.S. psychoanalyst and social philosopher (1900–1980) who explored the interaction between psychology and society. By applying psychoanalytic principles to the remedy of cultural ills, he believed humankind could develop a psychologically balanced "sane society."

34. There Is No Humor Here

The American writer and humorist (1835–1910) quoted in this puzzle published books characterized by broad, often irreverent, humor or biting social satire. He hated hypocrisy and oppression.

35. A Long Horn

In the novel quoted here, a creature begins a journey, determined to discover where the rest of the beings like her have gone.

36. Evolution

Human Knowledge

37. This is from an epic novel of humanity's first encounter with alien life. Hint: Ѧ stands for more than one English letter.

38. The Universe Within

The author of the quotation in the following cryptorune was a celebrated mystic (1342–1416) whose *Revelations of Divine Love* is one of the most remarkable documents of medieval religious experience. She spent the latter part of her life as a recluse at Saint Julian's Church in Norwich, England. In 1373, she became seriously ill but was healed after experiencing visions of Christ's suffering and of the Blessed Virgin. Unparalleled in English religious literature, *Revelations* deals with the most profound Christian mysteries, including the problems of predestination, the foreknowledge of God, and the existence of evil. The writer's sharp perceptions and her sincere, beautiful expression reveal a mind of awesome strength and charm.

Hint: the 26 characters in the Uvezich overdrive cipher look like the following:

Some of the symbols may fall on top of one another. For example, the two adjacent symbols and – combine to form: . Good luck with this brain-crusher!

39. Playing with Light

This quotation comes from the author of the Earthsea cycle, which has become one of the best-loved fantasies of our time. The windswept world of Earthsea is often compared with J. R. R. Tolkien's Middle Earth or C. S. Lewis's Narnia. In the Earthsea trilogy, the magic has gone out of the world. All over Earthsea the mages have forgotten their spells. This is the tale of a harrowing journey beyond the shores of death to heal a wounded land.

Hint: In the twenty-six-character Talethior cipher, characters look like this:

This means that a few letters in English will have the same symbol. For example, stands for two different English letters. Note that certain English letters will be represented by small accentlike marks. For example, the three adjacent symbols will look like when next to one another in the cipher. When adjacent, certain "accent" characters, like, collapse into a single character,. No one said this was going to be easy!

40. Suffering

This quotation is from a powerful book, set in a medieval fantasy world, demonstrating the power of myth and religion.

Hint: The twenty-six characters of the Kathasa catastrophe cipher look like this:

This code is a killer to crack because several characters, such as Π, –, ‘, and 3, stand for more than one English letter. Do you think anyone on this planet can decode the following?

41. Look Outward

This was written by Italy's greatest poet (1265–1321), one of the towering figures in western European literature.

42. Metallic Love

The American author of this line was a journalist, playwright, and children's fiction writer born in 1856. His father was a barrel maker who subsequently went into the oil business and became wealthy. The author's most famous work, written in 1900, has influenced American popular culture and imagination through books, film, song, and its philosophy of innocence and optimism.

43. Four Chambers

44. Beauty

This passage is by an Englishman (1885–1930) whose novels, short stories, poems, plays, essays, travel books, and letters made him one of the most influential writers of the twentieth century.

45. Who Owns Our Thoughts?

46. Be Happy

This advice comes from the progenitor of all people-skills books, first published in 1937. It was an overnight hit, eventually selling 15 million copies. The author believed that financial success was due 15 percent to professional knowledge and 85 percent to "the ability to express ideas, to assume leadership, and to arouse enthusiasm among people."

47. Acceptance

48. The Importance of the Heart

This passage was written by a French aviator and author whose beautiful books sometimes looked at adventure and danger with a poetic insight. He died in 1944, on a flight over the Mediterranean.

49. The Mystery of Love

50. Quiet Affection

An Italian tragic poet (1749–1803) who believed in the overthrow of tyranny wrote this.

51. Perseverance

52. Memory

The American anthropologist, educator, and author (1907–1977) quoted here wrote about anthropology for the layperson in a mystical, poetic style.

53. Christianity and Peace

This quotation is by a prolific American writer (1907–1988), one of the most literary authors of science fiction. His first story, "Life-Line," was published in the action-adventure pulp magazine *Astounding Science Fiction*.

54. Grasshopper Visions

The American novelist and short story writer (1916–1965) quoted here often dealt with the evil and chaos beneath the surface of ordinary, everyday life. Her chilling and much-debated tale "The Lottery" was first published in the *New Yorker* in 1948.

55. Kindness

This was written by one of the most influential science fiction writers of all time. Since his death in 1982, his novels and short stories have became more popular, thanks in part to two films based on his work: *Bladerunner,* from the novel *Do Androids Dream of Electric Sheep?* and the blockbuster *Total Recall,* inspired by the short story "We Can Remember It for You Wholesale." He probably had epilepsy and hypergraphia. From age fifteen, he suffered from auditory and visual hallucinations that he interpreted as signs from God. He also had macropsia and micropsia (the perception that stationary objects such as chairs are larger or smaller than they actually are), and depersonalization. Many of his symptoms found their way into his books as hallucinations experienced by his characters. He published his first short story at age thirteen, wrote at incredible speed, and produced thousands of pages of hand-written journals in addition to his forty-one books.

56. Termination

This pithy line is by an American poet, playwright, teacher, and public official (1892–1982) concerned with liberal democracy.

57. Suspended Animation

My favorite poet from North Carolina writes extraordinary poems that explore love in its many permutations, from obsession to fear to soft pleasure.

58. Destiny

This statement is by a French Catholic writer (1885–1970) who won the 1952 Nobel Prize for literature. His works examine the ugly realities of modern life in the light of eternity. His gloomy novels are psychological dramas, often concerning a religious soul wrestling with the problems of sin and salvation.

59. Keys to Infinity

No author in history has played a bigger role in opening the West to Buddhism than the one quoted here.

60. Solitude

The quote that follows is from the mathematician, physicist, religious philosopher, and master of French prose who laid the foundation for the modern theory of probability and promoted the idea that God could be experienced through the heart rather than through reason.
Reminder: As is usual with this rune set, [rune] can stand for two different letters.

61. Return

62. The Ultimate Trip

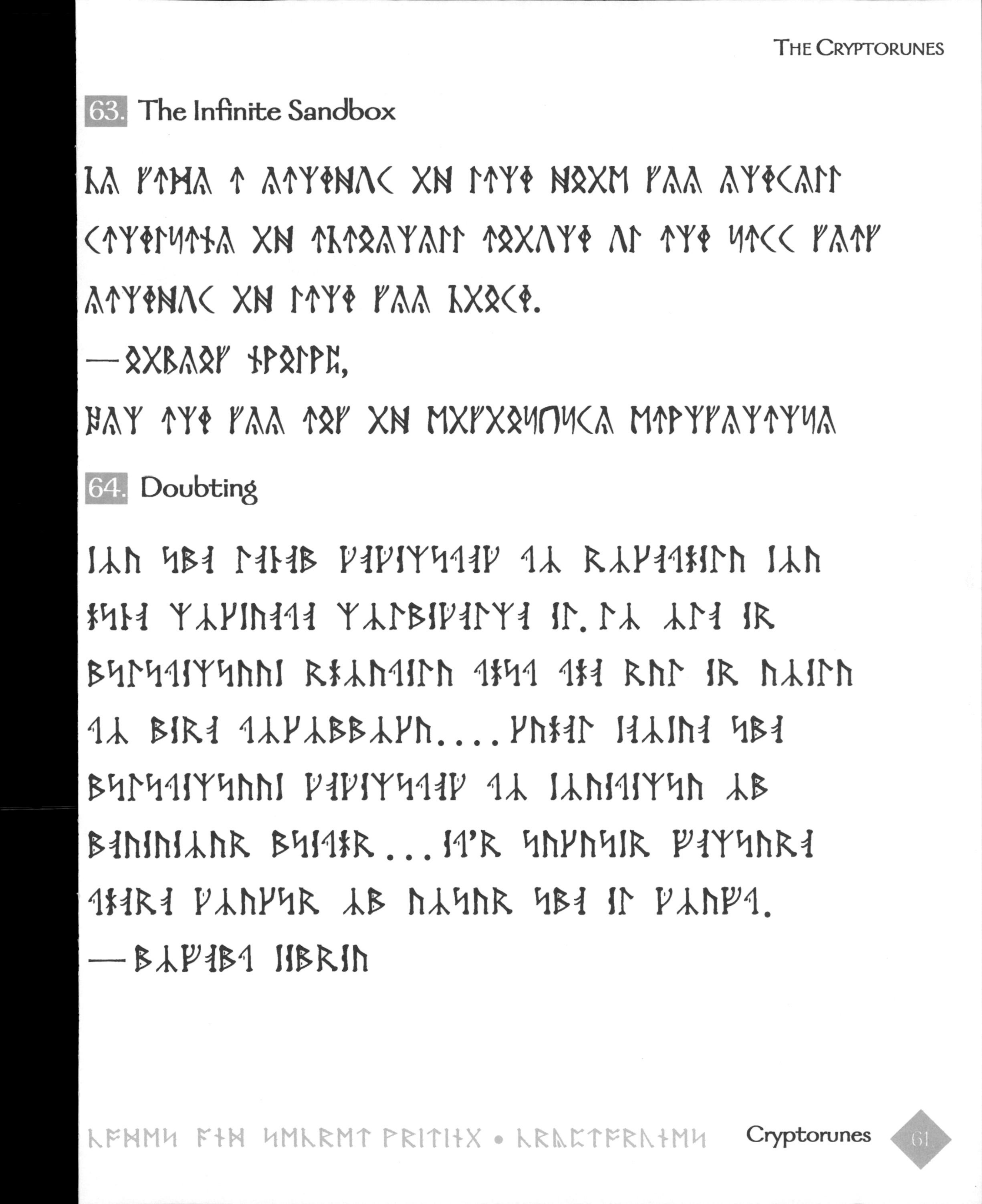

63. The Infinite Sandbox

64. Doubting

65. These Eyes

The French author (1871–1922) of the following quotation wrote the novel *Remembrance of Things Past,* a seven-volume work based on his life, recounted in psychological and allegorical terms.

66. Am I Dreaming?

This is from the works of a French poet, essayist, and critic (1871–1945) who was interested in scientific discoveries and political problems.

67. In the Woods

This quotation comes from an award-winning poet who is an associate professor in the department of English at Boston University.

68. Specialization

The Austrian zoologist (1903–1989) who wrote the following statement founded modern ethology, the study of animal behavior by means of comparative zoology. He showed how behavioral patterns may be traced to an evolutionary past, and he also studied the roots of aggression. In 1973, he shared the Nobel Prize for physiology and medicine with the animal behaviorists Karl von Frisch and Nikolaas Tinbergen.

69. Love and Happiness

70. Ocean Dreams

This is a passage by a French author (1828–1905) whose writings laid much of the foundation of modern science fiction.

71. Horse Sense

The novelist, playwright, and poet whose lines follow is the most important and celebrated author in Spanish literature. One of his novels has been translated, in whole or in part, into more than sixty languages. He lived from 1546 to 1616.

72. Randomness

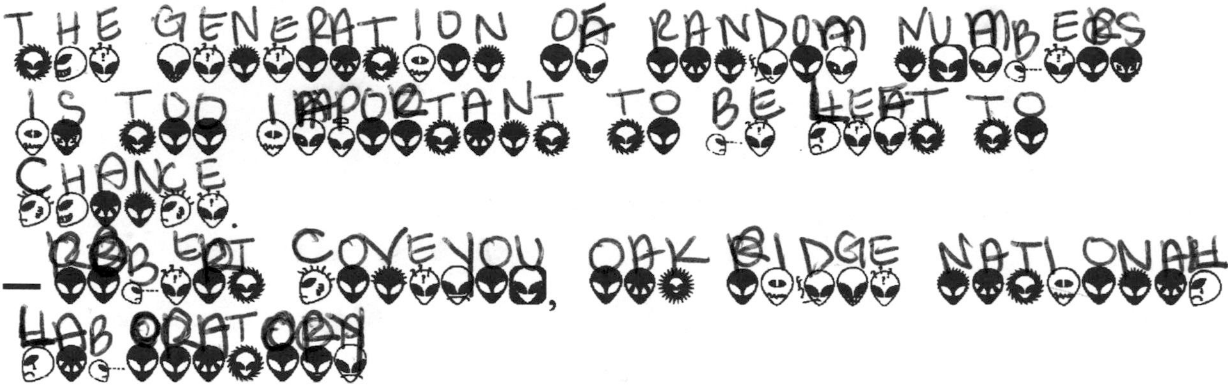

73. Thought and Vision

74. Thinking about Rocks

75. Land and Sea

This quotation is by American husband-and-wife writing collaborators, authors of the eleven-volume *Story of Civilization* (published 1935–1975), which established them as eminent writers of popular philosophy and history.

76. All Talk

This quotation comes from an English logician and philosopher best known for his work in mathematical logic and for his social and political campaigns. He advocated both pacifism and nuclear disarmament and received the Nobel Prize for literature in 1950.

77. Afterlife

Here is a quotation from the American politician and orator known as "the great agnostic," who popularized careful criticism of the Bible. He lived from 1833 to 1899, spending a significant portion of his life promoting humanistic philosophy and scientific rationalism.
Hint: the left-facing elephant is a period, the tiger is a comma, the crocodile is a semicolon.

78. Strange Patterns

The German-American physicist who wrote the next passage developed the special and general theories of relativity. He won the Nobel Prize for physics in 1921 for his explanation of the photoelectric effect.

79. Infinity

Here's a line by an English poet, dramatist, and actor who is considered by many the greatest dramatist of all time.

80. Difference

Born in 1945, one of today's most popular writers (author of over seventy novels, including many *New York Times* best-sellers) provided this statement.

ᛁᚷᛞᛞᛖ'ᛋ ᚹᛖᛖᚱ ᛁᚠᚳᛖᛋ, ᛏᛋᛏᚻᛁᚳ ᛁᚻᛁᛖ ᚻᛁ ᚱᚠᚢᚷᛁ ᚺᚷᛖᚱ ᚠ'ᚳ ᚻᛁᛈᚱᛖ, ᚺᚷᛖᚱ ᚠ'ᛉᛖ ᛁᚷᛈᛏᚢᚷᛁ ᛁᚷᛞᛞᛖ'ᛋ ᛋᛈᚳᛖᛁᚷᚠᚱᚢ ᚳᚠᛋᛋᚠᚱᚢ ᚠᚱ ᚳᛖ, ᛋᛈᚳᛖ ᛁᚠᚱᚳ ᛣᚠᛖᚹᛖ ᛁᚷᚻ'ᛋ ᚻᚱ ᛗᛋᛋᛗᚱᛁᚠᚻ ᛣᚻᛞᛁ ᛈᚴ ᚹᛖᚠᚱᚢ ᚷᛏᚳᚻᚱ. ᚠ'ᛉᛖ ᚴᛖᛁᛁ ᛏᚠᚴᚴᛖᛞᛖᚱᛁ ᚴᛞᛈᚳ ᛈᛁᚷᛖᛞ ᛣᛗᛈᛣᛁᛖ, ᚻᛁᚳᛈᛁ ᚻᛋ ᚠᚴ ᚠ'ᚳ ᚻ ᚳᛖᚳᚹᛖᛞ ᛈᚴ ᚻᚱᛈᛁᚷᛖᛞ ᛋᛣᛖᚹᚠᛖᛋ.

—ᛏᛖᚻᚱ ᛗᛈᛈᚱᛁᚠ, ᛁᚷᛖ ᚷᛈᛏᛋᛖ ᛈᚴ ᛁᚷᛏᚱᛏᛖᛞ

81. Existence

This piece of writing is by one of the most beloved personalities in the areas of recreational mathematics, magic, and puzzles. He is the author of more than sixty-five books and countless articles, on topics that include science, mathematics, philosophy, literature, and conjuring.
Hint: ·⁝· and ·⁚· are punctuation marks.

ᚦᛡᛁ ᛁᚹᚦᛁᛉᛦᛘᛒ ᛩᛋᛉᛒᚼ ᛁᚹ'ᛯᚦᛯ·⁝· ᚦᛡᛁ ᛯᚦᛉᚢᛕᚦᚢᛉᛁ ᛋᚱ ᚦᛡᛁ ᛩᛋᛉᛒᚼ 'ᛯ ᛋᛉᚼᛁᛉᛁᚼ·⁝· ᛩᛁ ᚽᛦᛋᛩ ᛒ'ᚦᚦᛒᛁ ᛘᛰᛋᚢᚦ ᚦᛡᛁ ᛦᛘᚦᚢᛉᛁ ᛋᚱ ᚦᛡᛁ ᛋᛉᚼᛁᛉ·⁚· ᛦᛋᚦᛡ'ᛦᛕ ᛘᚦ ᛘᛒᛒ ᛘᛰᛋᚢᚦ ᛩᛡᛒ 'ᚦ ᛯᛡᛋᚢᛒᚼ ᛁᚹ'ᛯᚦ.

—ᛁᛘᛉᚦ'ᛦ ᚹᛘᛉᚼᛦᛁᛉ·⁚· ᛋᛉᚼᛁᛉ ᛘᛦᚼ ᛯᚢᛉᛕᛉ'ᛯᛁ

82. Freedom

This quotation is by the first practicing psychiatrist (that is, someone with an M.D. degree and experience as a therapist) to host a radio show. He died in Los Angeles in 1995 of an apparent heart attack at age fifty-eight. Known for his tough way of questioning callers, whom he sometimes interrupted with an abrupt diagnosis, he said his method was based on three elements: speed, simplicity, and a relentless pursuit of truth.

83. The Seen and Unseen

In his time, the author of this quotation was the foremost prose satirist in the English language. His most famous work was *Gulliver's Travels,* published in 1726.

84. How Fast Can We Go?

85. Journey

Formerly chief of staff at the Boston Regional Medical Center, the physician quoted here also taught at Tufts University and Boston University Schools of Medicine and built a successful endocrinology practice in Boston. In 1992, he served on the National Institutes of Health Ad Hoc Panel on Alternative Medicine. Nearly ten million copies of his books have been sold in English alone. His best-sellers include *Ageless Body, Timeless Mind.*

86. Unfold

This quotation is by an author of numerous books, many of which are set in New Orleans. Her most famous book is *Interview with the Vampire.*

87. Mystery and Beauty

Hint: In this difficult cryptorune, letters sometimes appear to be composed of several symbols. For example, is a three-letter word composed of the composite symbols , , and .

88. You Will Know

From the *New York Times* best-selling author of *Jonathan Livingston Seagull* comes an inspirational account of an encounter with a modern-day messiah. The author takes to the air to show us that people don't need airplanes to soar.

89. Chaotic Love

This is from a horror novel that centers around a physicist and serial killer.

90. Angels

The Austro-German poet whose passage is quoted here became internationally famous with such works as *Duino Elegies* and *Sonnets to Orpheus*.

91. Fractal Birds

This quotation comes from an American biologist recognized as the world's leading expert on ants. He is also one of the main proponents of sociobiology, the study of the genetic basis of the social behavior.

92. Creation

Hint: In this cryptorune, letters sometimes touch in devilishly difficult ways. For example, the symbol is actually two separate symbols, and, that touch.

93. The Crystal Within

This passage was written by a practicing psychiatrist and past-life skeptic who was amazed when one of his patients seemed to recount past-life experiences.

94. Endless Horizons

This statement is by a previous president of the American Association for the Advancement of Sciences.

95. Physical Laws

This passage is by a major writer in the cyberpunk genre, the author of *Snow Crash*. In the novel from which this quotation is taken, the author imagines a future ruled by a rebirth of Victorian thinking. The main character is a brilliant technologist who dares to rebel against such regression.

ᛒᚨᚼᛣ ᚻᚳ ᛉᛦᛉᛣᛏᛚᛣ ᚨᛞᛗ ᚹᚨᚱᛦᚢᚹᚨᚱᛏᛚᛣ ᚨᚴᚢ ᛒᛏᚺᚢ
ᚨ ᛚᚻᚻᚴᛗᛏᛞᚨᚱᚢ ᛣᛉᛣᚱᚢᚹ ᚱᛦᚨᚱ ᚴᚥᛞᛣ ᛏᛞ ᚻᛞᛒᛉ
ᚻᛞᚢ ᛗᛏᚹᚢᛞᛣᛏᚻᛞ. ᛉᚢᚴᛦᚨᛉᛣ ᚱᛦᚢᚴᚢ ᛏᛣ ᚨᛞᚻᚱᛦᚢᚴ
ᛗᛏᚹᚢᛞᛣᛏᚻᛞ ᛉᚢᚴᛉᚢᛞᛗᛏᛚᚥᛒᚨᚴ ᚱᚻ ᛏᚱ, ᛏᛞᚾᛏᛣᛏᚻᛒᚢ
ᚱᚻ ᚱᛦᚻᛣᚢ ᛒᚨᚼᛣ ᚻᚳ ᛉᛦᛉᛣᛏᛚᛣ, ᛗᚢᛣᛚᚴᛏᚻᛏᛞᚷ ᚱᛦᚢ
ᛣᚨᚹᚢ ᚱᛦᛏᛞᚷᛣ ᚼᛏᚱᛦ ᛗᛏᚳᚳᚢᚴᚢᛞᚱ ᚴᚥᛒᚢᛣ, ᚨᛞᛗ
ᚱᛦᚻᛣᚢ ᚴᚥᛒᚢᛣ ᚨᚴᚢ ᚼᚴᛏᚱᚱᚢᛞ ᛏᛞ ᚻᚥᚴᛦᚢᚨᚴᚱᛣ, ᛏᛞ
ᚨ ᛗᚢᚢᛉ ᛉᛒᚨᛚᚢ ᚼᛦᚢᚴᚢ ᚼᚢ ᛚᚨᛞᛞᚻᚱ ᚷᚻ ᚨᛞᛗ ᚴᚢᚨᛗ
ᚱᛦᚢᚹ ᚢᛈᛚᚢᛉᚱ ᛏᛞ ᚻᚥᚴ ᛗᚴᚢᚨᚹᛣ.

—ᛞᚢᚨᛒ ᛣᚱᚢᛉᛦᚢᛞᛣᚻᛞ, ᚱᛦᚢ ᛗᛏᚨᚹᚻᛞᛗ ᚨᚷᚢ

96. Sharing

In the novel quoted here, the creator of *2001: A Space Odyssey* teams up with a space scientist to give readers an exciting science fiction adventure. An alien creature is dormant at the bottom of the ocean. Then the creature awakens.

97. Marital Bliss

Here's an epigram by an American oil billionaire reputed to be the richest man in the world at the time of his death. He owned a controlling interest in a large oil company and nearly 200 other businesses.

98. Stranger

This passage was written by a French novelist, essayist, and playwright best known for such novels as *The Stranger* (published in 1942). He received the 1957 Nobel Prize for literature.

99. Eternity

This narrative is from my favorite history book. First published in 1921, the volume has charmed generations of readers with its warmth, simplicity, and wisdom. It begins with the origins of human life and sweeps forward to illuminate all of history.

100. Staying Home

A Czech-born German-language writer of visionary fiction wrote the piece of advice that follows. His novels express the anxieties and alienation of twentieth-century humanity.

ᛋᛒᚦ ᛐᛒ ᛦᛒᛁ ᛦᛘᛘᛐ ᛁᛒ ᛉᛘᚽᛯᛘ ᛋᛒᚦᛑ ᛑᛒᛒᚠ. ᛑᛘᚠᚽᚿᛦ
ᛌᚿᛁᛁᚿᛦᚢ ᚽᛁ ᛋᛒᚦᛑ ᛁᚽᚹᛉᛘ ᚽᛦᛐ ᛉᚿᛌᛁᛘᛦ. ᛐᛒ ᛦᛒᛁ ᛘᛯᛘᛦ
ᛉᚿᛌᛁᛘᛦ, ᛌᚿᚠᛰᛉᛋ ᛯᚽᚿᛁ. ᛐᛒ ᛦᛒᛁ ᛘᛯᛘᛦ ᛯᚽᚿᛁ, ᚹᛘ ᚱᚦᚿᛁᛘ
ᛌᛁᚿᛉᛉ ᚽᛦᛐ ᛌᛒᛉᚿᛁᚽᛑᛋ. ᛁᚤᛘ ᛯᛒᛑᛉᛐ ᛯᚿᛉᛉ ᛚᛑᛘᛘᛉᛋ ᛒᛚᛚᛘᛑ
ᚿᛁᛌᛘᛉᛚ ᛁᛒ ᛋᛒᚦ ᛁᛒ ᚹᛘ ᚦᛦᚠᚽᛌᛂᛘᛐ, ᚿᛁ ᚤᚽᛌ ᛦᛒ ᚥᚤᛒᚿᚥᛘ,
ᚿᛁ ᛯᚿᛉᛉ ᛑᛒᛉᛉ ᚿᛦ ᛘᚥᛌᛁᚽᛌᛋ ᚽᛁ ᛋᛒᚦᛑ ᛚᛘᛘᛁ.

— ᛚᛑᚽᛦᛣ ᛂᚽᛚᛂᚽ

CHAPTER 5

THE GOLDEN RUNE CONTEST

Somewhere in this chapter are hidden clues about the locations of several marvelous golden runes. The runes hold the key to many of Earth's problems and answer some of the universe's deepest mysteries. One golden rune is hidden somewhere on Earth, back in time. Another is hidden in a crater on the moon. Can you find the clues to determine the exact locations of these runes and several others? If you can find at least four runes, send me their locations, and you will get a certificate, signed and numbered, attesting to your cryptorunic skills. See the reward offer at the end of this chapter for anyone solving all seventeen visitations. The visitations also give clues about the location of a supersecret golden rune hidden somewhere in the northeastern United States.

Imagine that, after a long ocean journey, you have arrived at the Peruvian coast and traveled inland. You are now exploring the Peruvian rain forest at the base of Mount Huascarán, the highest mountain in Peru. Each day you receive a visit from a shaman, who hands you clay tablets with possible clues about the runes' locations. Get set for a mystical quest and adventure. The following visitations vary greatly in difficulty. Some go beyond simple substitution cryptograms. If you get stuck on one visitation, go to the next. Do not fear. The truth will freely offer itself to you to be unmasked. You have no choice. Your Peruvian shaman will roll in ecstasy at your feet.

Visitation 1

[illegible]

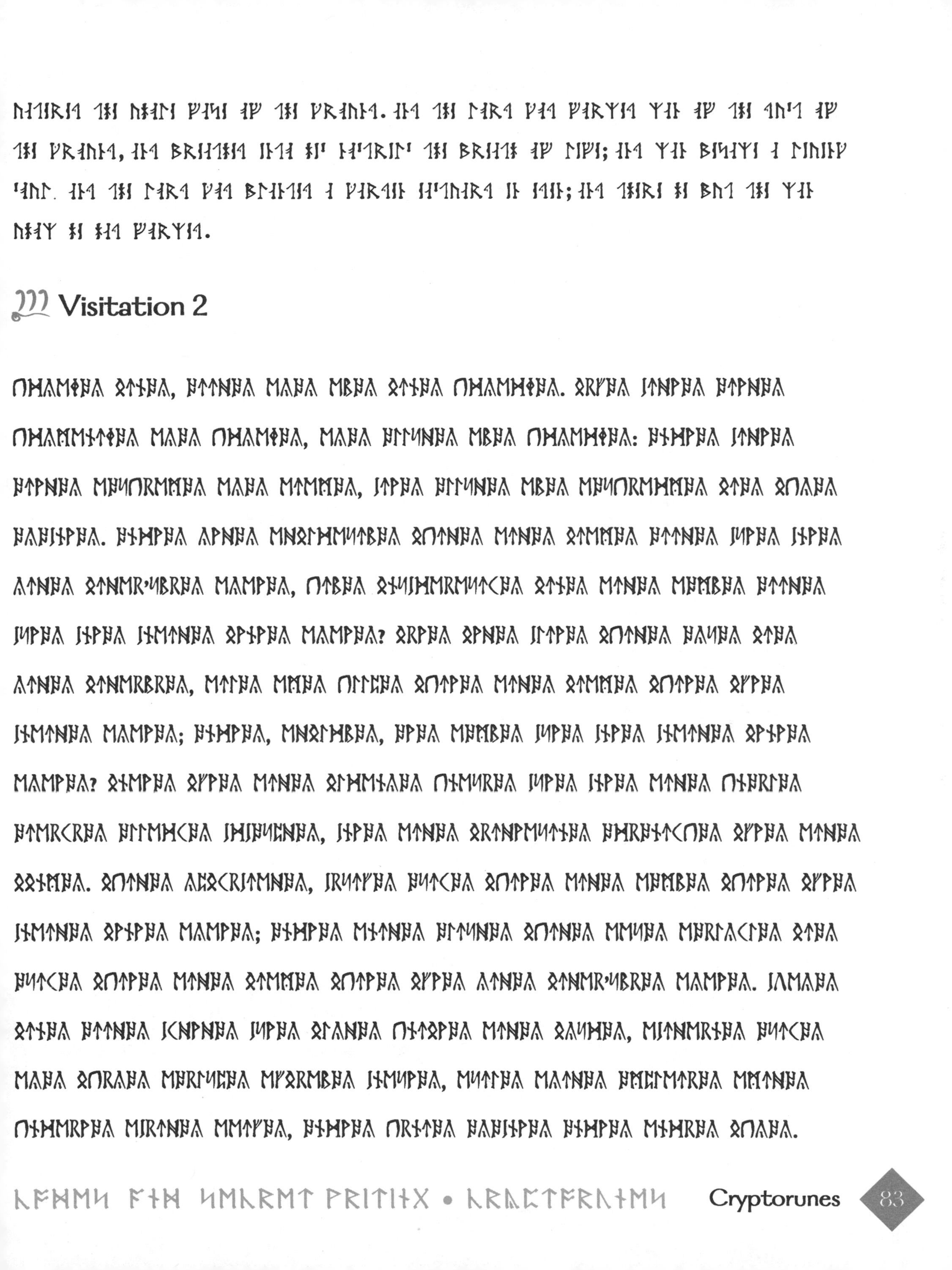

Visitation 2

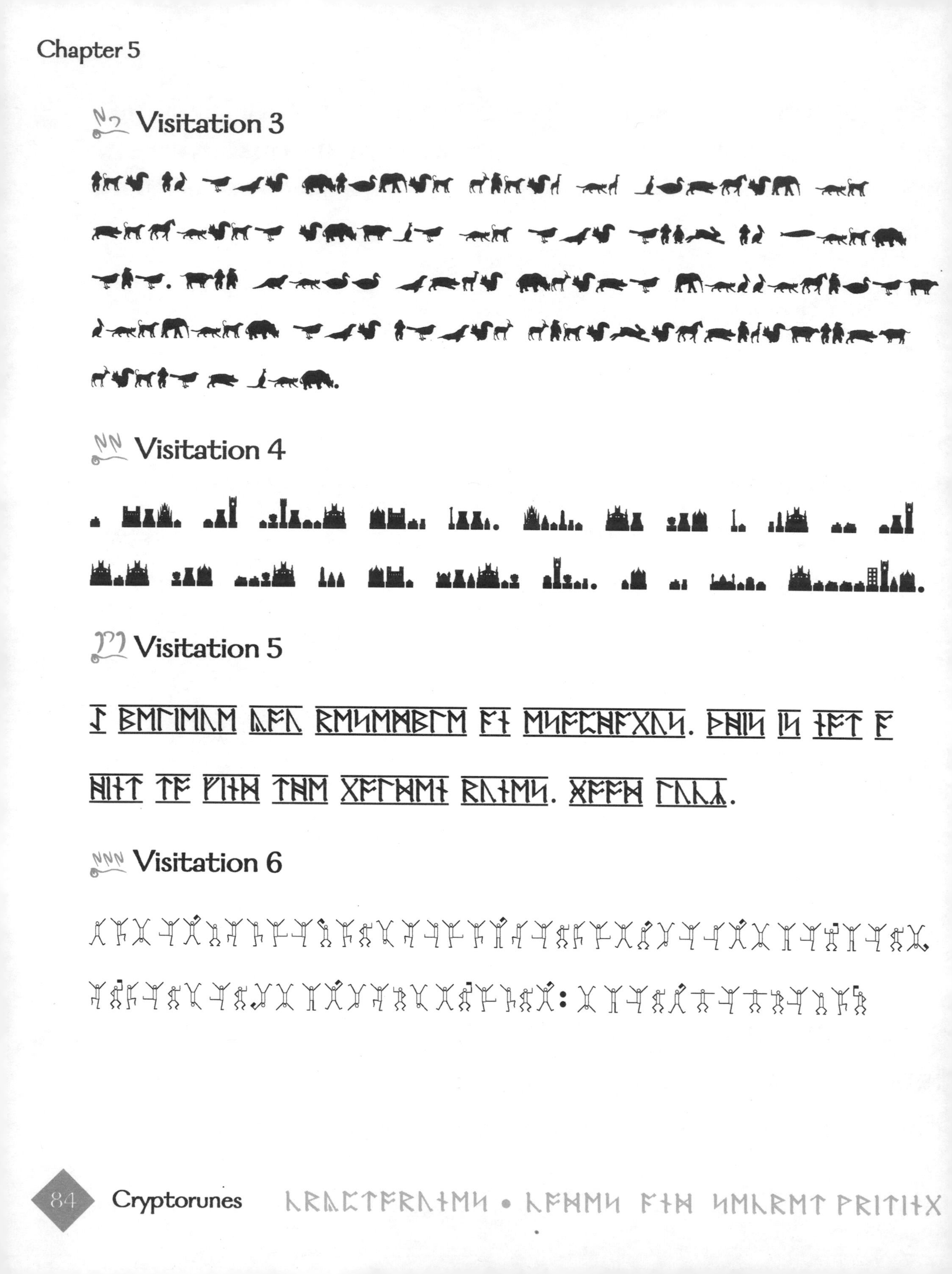

Visitation 3

Visitation 4

Visitation 5

Visitation 6

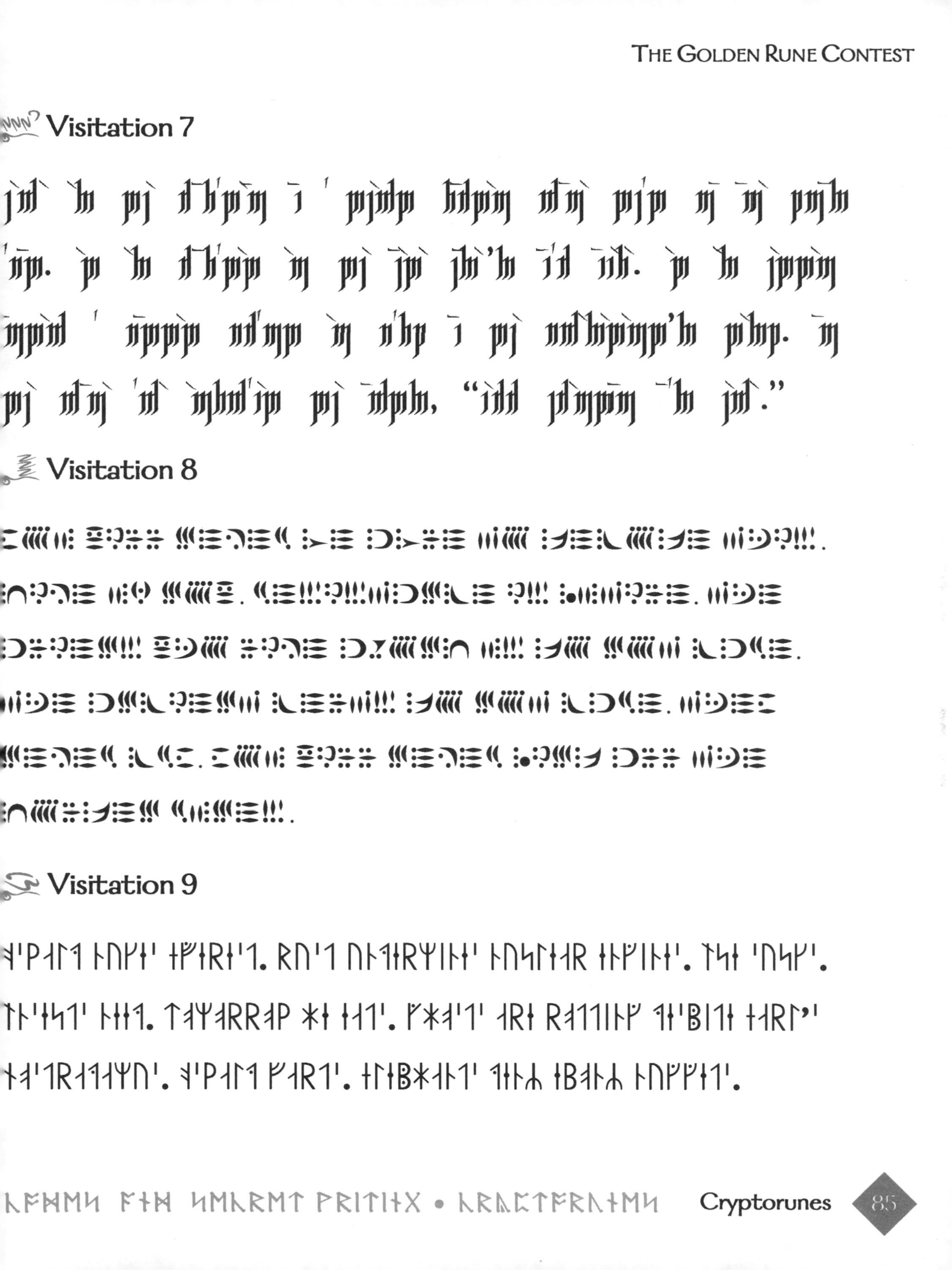

Visitation 7

Visitation 8

Visitation 9

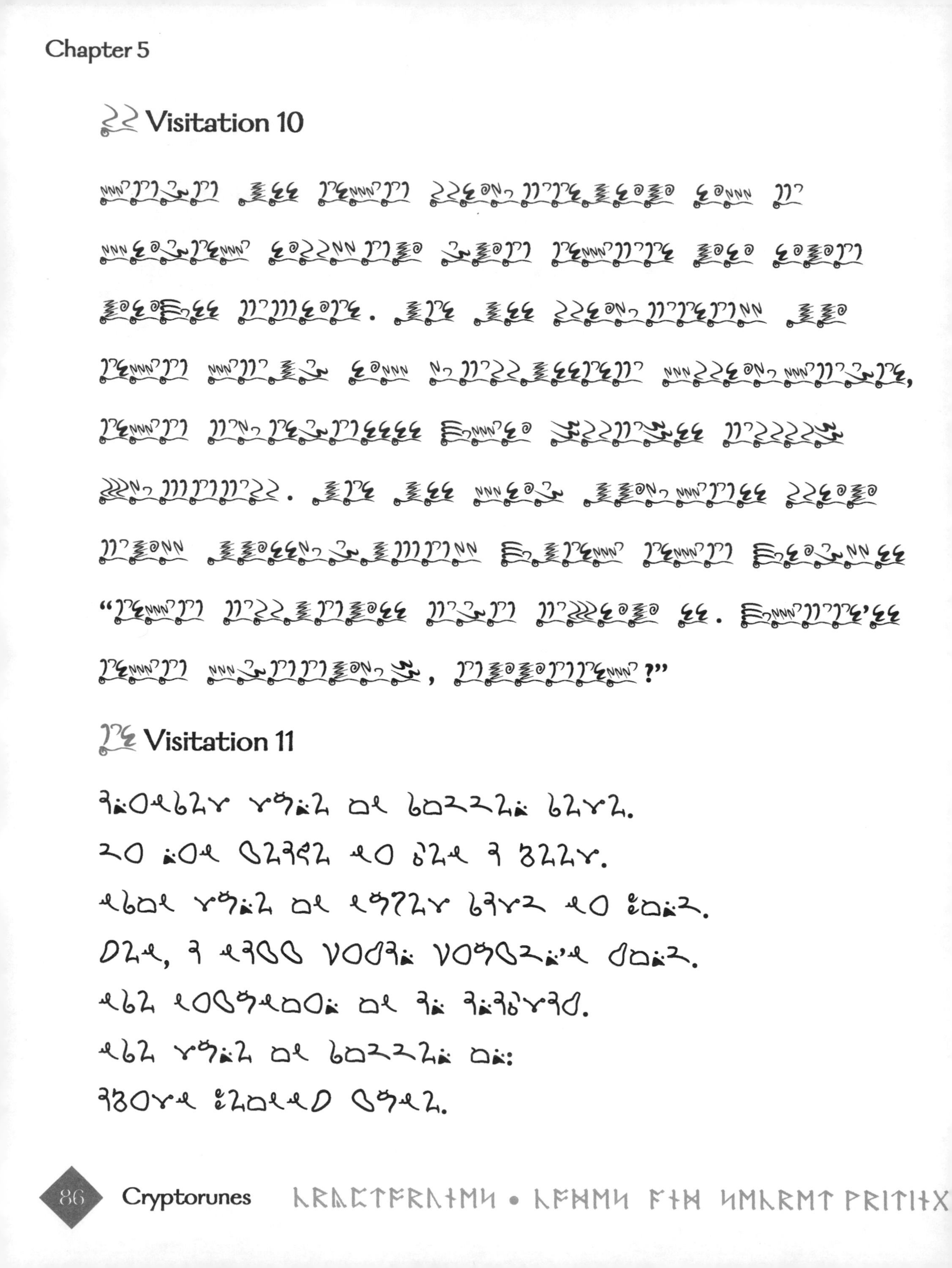

Visitation 10

Visitation 11

Visitation 12

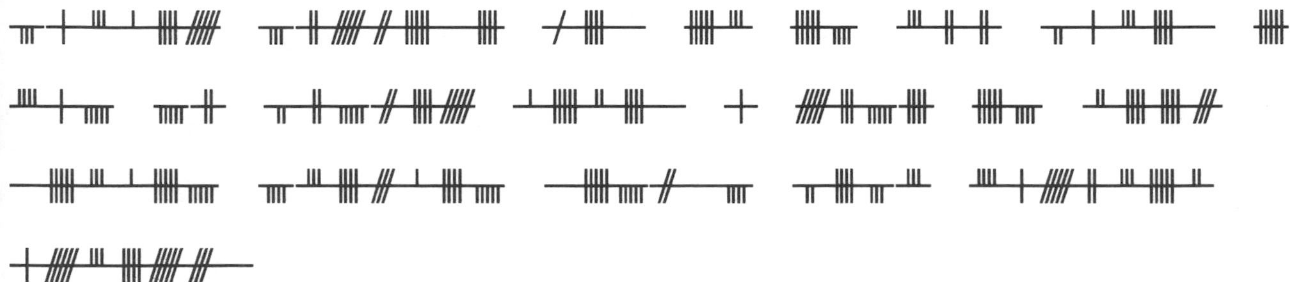

Visitation 13

Visitation 14

Visitation 15

Visitation 16

Visitation 17

Award Offer!

As a reward to the first five people with the awesome ability to completely decipher the meaning of all seventeen visitations, I offer a magnificent set of twenty-five rune stones, a velvet pouch with drawstring, and a rune chart. Write to me with solutions: Clifford Pickover, P.O. Box 549, Millwood, New York 10546-0549, USA. CIA analysts, quantum cryptographers, and their families are excluded from the contest. (Just kidding; anyone can try.) Progress reports may be found at www.pickover.com.

CHAPTER 6

CLUES

This section offers a single clue, or letter equivalent, for each puzzle in chapter 4. If ᚻ equals *A* in a cryptorune, then ᚻ will equal *A* throughout that cryptorune. However, in a few instances, a single rune can stand for two or three letters. Since each cryptorune has its own code, the clue and letter equivalents will be different in each puzzle.

1. ᛕᚹ = I
2. ᛉ = I
3. X̄ = W
4. ↑ = S
5. ᛘ = A
6. ᛯ = W
7. ᛖ = T
8. ᛩ = D
9. ᚽ = A
10. ᛈ = L
11.] = I
12. ᛀ = Y
13. ᛒ = Y
14. ᛕ = B
15. ᚺ = W
16. ᛦ̲ = T
17. ᛒ = A
18. ᛝ = W
19. ᛊ = I
20. M̄ = E
21. ᚨ = I
22. ᛦ = I
23. ᛘ̲ = T
24. ᚠ = T
25. ᛈ = D
26. ✳ = L
27. R̄ = O
28. 𓃥 = D
29. ᛉ = T
30. ᛚ = I
31. ᛉ = H
32. ᛚ = T
33. ᛕᚹ = T
34. ᛘ̲ = G
35. ᛯ = O
36. ♠ = D
37. ᚹ = C
38. Ƶ = H
39. ` = H
40. Ȝ = W
41. Ձ = T
42. Λ = N
43. ˈ = A
44. ♠ = E
45. h = T
46. ƛ = T
47. ђ = A
48. ʊ = T
49. ˈ = A
50. ᛦ̲ = T
51. ⊠ = D
52. ᛩ = L
53. ⁝Ɔ = M
54. ↿ = N
55. ᛘ = T
56. ᛒ = A
57. ᚹ = U
58. ᛚ = W
59. ● = T
60. ᛞ = T
61. ᚼ̲ = T
62. ■ = T
63. ƛ = W
64. ⌡ = Y
65. Ч̄ = T
66. ᚠ = T
67. | = T
68. R = E
69. ≈ = L
70. ▴ = I
71. ᛦ = H
72. ✪ = T
73. X = T
74. ᛚ = A
75. X̄ = H
76. ᛯ = M
77. ♠ = L
78. ■ = W
79. ↑ = I
80. | = T
81. þ = T
82. ᚼ̲ = S
83. ʊ = V
84. ᛚ = O
85. Ʒ = I
86. ʒ = W
87. ⁝∩ = T
88. ᛒ = A
89. ɱ = C
90. ⊥ = W
91. ᛉ = I
92. ᘐ = I
93. ɱ = I
94. ʃ = W
95. ᛒ = L
96. — = W
97. ᚠ = A
98. ▲ = I
99. ᛯ = T
100. Ч = Y

CHAPTER 7
SOLUTIONS

Alien Anagram: The solution to the alien anagram in chapter 1 is given in the following code. (You didn't think I would make it *that* easy for you, considering that no one has ever cracked this anagram!)

ᛡᚽᚱᚽ ᛁ' ᛏᛡᚽ 'ᚭᚴᚢᛏᛁᚭᚿ ᛏᚭ ᛏᛡᚽ ᚭᚴᛁᚽᚿ
ᚭᚿᚭᚹᚱᚭᛘ. ᛏᚱᛦ ᛁᛏ ᚭᚿ ᛦᚭᚢᚱ ᚠᚱᛁᚽᚿᛑ'.
ᛏᛡᚽ ᚭᚿ'ᚹᚽᚱ ᛁ': "ᚹᚽ ᚴᚭᚹᚽ ᛒᚭᛒᛋᚭᚱᚿ."

Lincos: In chapter 3, we discussed Hans Freudenthal's Lincos language, explained in his book *Lincos: Design of a Language for Cosmic Intercourse,* published in the Netherlands in 1960. The three-letter symbols are derived from Latin roots. For example, *Fem* means "female"; *Msc* means "male." Here is a decoding of the message:

> The existence of the human body begins some time earlier than that of the human itself. The same is true for animals. Mat, mother. Pat, father. Before the individual existence of a human, its body is part of the body of its mother. It has originated from a part of the body of its mother and a part of the body of its father.

Not very intuitive, is it?

Cryptorunes: The following are full solutions to all the cryptorunes in chapter 4. Don't peek until you have spent at least ten minutes on a cryptorune.

1. If we wish to understand the nature of the universe we have an inner hidden advantage: we are ourselves little portions of the universe and so carry the answer within us.
—Jacques Boivin, *The Single Heart Field Theory*

2. I just hope that I can laugh through all phases of life, live to a very ripe old age, and leave the body behind like slipping off a tight shoe. —Clay Fried

3. We wander as children through a cave; yet though the way be lost, we journey from the darkness to the light. —The Gospel according to Thomas XV:I

4. Surely it heard me cry out—for at that moment, like two exploding white stars, the hands flashed open and the figure dropped back into the earth, back to the kingdom, older than ours, that calls the dark its home. —*Children of the Kingdom,* T. E. D. Kline

5. As one goes through it, one sees that the gate one went through was the self that went through it.
—R. D. Laing

6. Whoever feels the touch of my hand shall become as I am, and hidden things shall be revealed to him . . . I am the All, and the All came forth from me. Cleave a piece of wood and you will find me; lift up a stone and I am there.
—The Gospel according to Thomas

7. The Buddha, the Godhead, resides quite as comfortably in the circuits of a digital computer or the gears of a cycle transmission as he does at the top of a mountain or in the petals of a flower; to think otherwise is to demean the Buddha—which is to demean oneself. —Robert Pirsig, *Zen and the Art of Motorcycle Maintenance*

8. Death is passing on—the making way of life and time for life. Hate dying and killing, not death. —S. R. Donaldson, *Lord Foul's Bane*

9. A place is nothing: not even space, unless at its heart, a figure stands. —Paul Dirac

10. Love with care—and then what you will, do. —St. Augustine

11. It is God that girdeth me with strength. . . . He teacheth my hands to war. —Psalm 18:32, 34

12. You are so part of the world that your slightest action contributes to its reality. Your breath changes the atmosphere. Your encounters with others alter the fabrics of their lives, and the lives of those who come in contact with them. —Jane Roberts

13. You have said that the land is a dream for you—and that you fear to be made mad. But madness is not the only danger in dreams. There is also the danger that something may be lost which can never be regained. —S. R. Donaldson, *Lord Foul's Bane*

14. Be still, heart: make no expostulation. Hold peace and grief, and be still. —S. R. Donaldson, *Lord Foul's Bane*

15. We fear death, yet we long for slumber and beautiful dreams. —Kahlil Gibran

16. The chasm was merely one of the orifices of that pit of blackness that lies beneath us, everywhere. —S. R. Donaldson, *Lord Foul's Bane*

17. And what is love without the eternal enmity between the sexes. —Hermann Hesse

18. When the mind is lost, it finds solace in a new world. —Johann Goethe, *Faust*

19. I am become death, the shatterer of worlds. —Krishna to the Prince, *The Bhagavad Gita*

20. Every time a child says "I don't believe in fairies" there is a fairy somewhere that falls down dead. —James Matthew Barrie

21. I looked round the trees. The thin net of reality. These trees, this sun. I was infinitely far from home. The profoundest distances are never geographical. —John Fowles, *The Magus*

22. I am half inclined to think we are all ghosts. . . . They are not actually alive in us; but there they are dormant, all the same, and we can never be rid of them. Whenever I take up a newspaper and read it, I fancy I see ghosts creeping between the lines. There must be ghosts all over the world. They must be as countless as grains of sand it seems to me. And we are so miserably afraid of the light, all of us. —Henrik Ibsen

23. There are times when silence is a poem. —John Fowles, *The Magus*

24. The conditions of a solitary bird are five: First, that it flies to the highest point. Second, that it does not suffer for company, not even of its own kind. Third, that it aims its beak to the sky. Fourth, that it does not have a definite color. Fifth, that it sings very softly. —Carlos Castaneda, *Tales of Power*

25. Did we come here to laugh or cry? Are we dying or being born? —Carlos Fuentes, *Terra Nostra*

26. Life survives in the chaos of the cosmos by picking order out of the winds. Death is certain, but life becomes possible by following patterns that lead like paths of firmer ground through the swamps of time. Cycles of light and dark, of heat and cold, of magnetism, radioactivity, and gravity all provide vital guides—and life learns to respond to even their most subtle signs. The emergence of a fruitfly is tuned by a spark lasting one thousandth of a second; the breeding of a bristleworm is coordinated on the ocean floor by a glimmer of light reflected from the moon. . . . Nothing happens in isolation. We breathe and bleed, we laugh and cry, we crash and die in time with cosmic cues. —Lyall Watson, *Supernature*

27. Our normal waking consciousness is but one special type of consciousness, whilst all about it, parted from it by the filmiest of screens, there lie potential forms of consciousness entirely different. No account of the universe in its totality can be final which leaves these other forms of consciousness quite disregarded. They may determine attitudes though

they cannot furnish formulas, and open a region though they fail to give a map.
—William James, *The Varieties of Religious Experience*

28. Do not hurt where holding is enough; do not wound where hurting is enough; do not maim where wounding is enough; and kill not where maiming is enough. The greatest warrior is he who does not need to kill. —S. R. Donaldson, *Lord Foul's Bane*

29. The bird fights its way out of the egg. The egg is the world. Who would be born must first destroy a world. The bird flies to God. That God's name is Abraxas. —Hermann Hesse, *Demian*

30. I can show you fear in a handful of dust. —T. S. Eliot

31. Human territory is defined least of all by physical frontiers. —John Fowles, *The Magus*

32. These are the pale deaths which men miscall their lives. For all the scents of green things growing, each breath is but an exhalation of the grave. Bodies jerk like puppet corpses, and hell walks laughing.
—S. R. Donaldson, *Lord Foul's Bane*

33. The deepest need of man is to overcome his separateness, to leave the prison of his aloneness.
—Eric Fromm, *The Art of Loving*

34. God is a comedian playing to an audience which doesn't laugh. —Mark Twain

35. Only that which can die is beautiful.
—P. Beagle, *The Last Unicorn*

36. Descended from monkeys? My dear let us hope that is not true! But if it is true, let us hope that it not become widely known! —The wife of the bishop of Worcester, upon hearing Charles Darwin's theory of evolution through natural selection

37. Consider the true picture. Think of myriads of tiny bubbles, very sparsely scattered, rising through a vast black sea. We rule some of the bubbles. Of the waters we know nothing . . . . —Larry Niven and Jerry Pournelle, *The Mote in God's Eye*

38. He showed me a little thing, the quantity of a hazelnut, in the palm of my hand, and it was round as a ball. I looked thereupon with the eye of my understanding and thought: What may this be? And it was answered generally thus: It is all that is made.
—Julian of Norwich, 14th century

39. He stopped, for saying the truth aloud was unendurable. He knew now why this tranquil life seemed like an after-life or a dream, unreal. It was because he knew in his heart that reality was empty: without life or warmth or color or sound: without meaning. There were no heights or depths. All this lovely play of form and light and color on the sea and in the eyes of men was no more than that: a playing of illusions on the shallow void.
—Ursula K. Le Guin, *The Farthest Shore*

40. Who can describe the course of suffering to the end where no more can be endured? Who can express the unendurable vision of a world created solely for horror and torment—the struggling of the half-crushed beetle glued to the ground by its own entrails, the flapping, broken fish pecked to death by gulls upon the sand; the dying ape filled with maggots, the young soldier, eviscerated screaming in the arms of his comrades; the child who weeps alone, wounded for life by the desertion of those who have gone their selfish ways? Save us, O God, only place us where we may see the sun and eat a little bread until it is time to die, and we ask nothing more. And when the snake devours the fallen fledgling before our eyes, then our indifference is Thy mercy. —Richard Adams, *Shardik*

41. The heavens call to you, and circle about you, displaying to you their eternal splendors, and your eye gazes only to earth. —Dante

42. Now I know I have a heart, because it's breaking. —Last words of the Tin Man to Dorothy, *The Wizard of Oz*

43. A heart is not measured by how much one loves, but by how much one is loved by others.
—L. Frank Baum, *The Wizard of Oz*

44. Everything that has beauty has a body, and is a body; everything that has being has being in the flesh: and dreams are only drawn from bodies that are.
—D. H. Lawrence, "Bodiless God"

45. The dreams of men belong to God.
—S. R. Donaldson, *Lord Foul's Bane*

46. The best cure for depression is achievement.
—Dale Carnegie, *How to Win Friends and Influence People*

47. Accepting a gift honors the giver.
—S. R. Donaldson

48. That which is essential is invisible to the eye. . . . It is only with the heart that one sees rightly. —Antoine de Saint-Exupéry, *The Little Prince*

49. And once, when I rose from your body, it was like water I had looked into, water I had held. —Stanley Plimly, "Out of the Body Travel"

50. There is silence born of love, which expresses everything. —Conte Vittorio Alfieri

51. Do not follow where the path may lead. Go, instead, where there is no path and leave a trail. —Isaac Newton (I have doubts as to whether Newton actually said this. Can anyone confirm?)

52. Life is a movement from the forgotten into the unexpected. —Loren Eiseky, *The Immense Journey*

53. Maybe Jesus was right when he said that the meek shall inherit the earth—but they inherit very small plots about six feet by three. —Robert Heinlein, *Stranger in a Strange Land*

54. No live organism can continue for long to exist sanely under conditions of absolute reality. Even larks and katydids are supposed, by some, to dream. —Shirley Jackson, *The Haunting of Hill House*

55. The measure of man is not his intelligence. It is not how high he rises in this freakish establishment. The measure of man is this: How swiftly can he react to another person's need? And how much of himself can he give? —Philip K. Dick, *Our Friends from Frolix Eight*

56. A world ends when its metaphor has died. —Archibald MacLeish

57. Under this town's ashes lies a man, still sweating the long summer days, his body perfect as morning to the bacon and eggs in his belly. His skin is damp in the humid earth, closed eyes heavier under rain. The heart quit pumping early, but when a rock eases down and cuts an arm or grazes his back, blood still seeps from the veins, the clots blooming like poppies around him. In the brain memories lie opened, one into the other: the crunch of the ax as he swings down hard, his wife calling him in, a woman singing his name in the distance. He does not hear them, but they are there, claiming their portions. By now the wife may be dead too, the ax passed down to his son, or rusted under the woodpile. The woman cannot recall her own clear voice or the features of the man who should be bones. —Susan Bartels Ludvigson, "On Learning that Certain Peat Bogs Contain Perfectly Preserved Bodies"

58. We are all molded and remolded by those who have loved us and though that love may pass we remain, nonetheless, their work. No love, no friendship, can ever cross the path of our destiny without leaving some mark upon it forever. . . . —François Mauriac

59. There was from the very beginning no need for a struggle between the finite and infinite. The peace we are so eagerly seeking has been there all the time. —D. T. Suzuki, *Zen Buddhism*

60. The sole cause of man's unhappiness is that he does not know how to stay quietly in his own room. —Blaise Pascal

61. The end of all our explorations will be to come back to where we began and discover the place for the first time. —T. S. Eliot

62. True journey is return. —Ursula K. Le Guin, *A Wizard of Earthsea*

63. We take a handful of sand from the endless landscape of awareness around us and call that handful of sand the world. —Robert Pirsig, *Zen and the Art of Motorcycle Maintenance*

64. You are never dedicated to something you have complete confidence in. No one is fanatically shouting that the sun is going to rise tomorrow. . . . When people are fanatically dedicated to political or religious faiths . . . it's always because these dogmas or goals are in doubt. —Robert Pirsig

65. The most exotic journey would not be to see a thousand different places, but to see a single place through a thousand persons' eyes. —Marcel Proust

66. The best way to make your dreams come true is to wake up. —J. M. Power and Paul Valéry

67. The forest leans into the man's sleep. It cannot dream for itself. —Rosanna Warren, "The Field"

68. Every man gets a narrower and narrower field of knowledge in which he must be an expert in order to compete with other people. The specialist knows more and more about less and less and finally knows

everything about nothing. —Konrad Lorenz

69. Love is that condition in which the happiness of another person is essential to your own.
—Robert Heinlein

70. I am reminded of a French poet who, when asked why he took walks accompanied by a lobster with a blue ribbon around its neck, replied, "Because it does not bark, and because it knows the secret of the sea." —Jules Verne

71. He calmly rode on, leaving it to his horse's discretion to go which way it pleased, firmly believing that in this consisted the very essence of adventures.
—Miguel de Cervantes, *Don Quixote*

72. The generation of random numbers is too important to be left to chance. —Robert Coveyou, Oak Ridge National Laboratory

73. Thinking is more interesting than knowing, but less interesting than looking. —Wolfgang von Goethe

74. A rock pile ceases to be a rock pile the moment a single man contemplates it, bearing within him the image of a cathedral. —Antoine de Saint-Exupéry

75. History is subject to geology. Every day the sea encroaches somewhere upon the land, or the land upon the sea; cities disappear under the water, and sunken cathedrals ring their melancholy bells.
—Will and Ariel Durant, *The Lessons of History*

76. Mathematics is the only science where one never knows what one is talking about nor whether what is said is true. —Bertrand Russell

77. Life is a narrow vale between the cold and barren peaks of two eternities. We strive in vain to look beyond the heights. We cry aloud, and the only answer is the echo of our wailing cry. From the voiceless lips of the unreplying dead there comes no word; but in the night of death hope sees a star and listening love can hear the rustle of a wing.
—Robert G. Ingersoll, *The Ghosts and Other Lectures*

78. We are in the position of a little child entering a huge library whose walls are covered to the ceiling with books in many different tongues. The child does not understand the languages in which they are written. He notes a definite plan in the arrangement of books, a mysterious order which he does not comprehend, but only dimly suspects. —Albert Einstein

79. I could be bounded in a nutshell and count myself a king of infinite space.
—William Shakespeare, *Hamlet*

80. There's been times, usually late at night when I'm alone, when I've thought there's something missing in me, some tiny piece that's an essential part of being human. I've felt different from other people, almost as if I'm a member of another species.
—Dean Koontz, *The House of Thunder*

81. The external world exists; the structure of the world is ordered; we know little about the nature of the order, nothing at all about why it should exist.
—Martin Gardner, *Order and Surprise*

82. Sorrow ages you prematurely. When you're in emotional debt, you're pessimistic about the future, and even in your green years, long to return to the past to remedy the shortfalls of love and opportunity you suffered. Sometimes you yearn for more caring, for more time with someone who is no longer here, for a chance to speak your mind and release your emotional burden, or just to resolve your confusion by finally discovering what really happened to you. You can speculate, you can lament, you can yearn, but as much as you may wish to return and round off your emotional experience, you can never go home again. Your real home is in this place, at this time. The present is for action, for doing, for becoming, and for growing. —Dr. David Viscott, *Emotionally Free*

83. Vision is the art of seeing things invisible.
—Jonathan Swift

84. Of this we know, man can not travel faster than the speeding horse, for his frame is too delicate to sustain such speeds and not perish.
—J. Harold Smith, physician, 1892

85. I don't need to know where I'm going to enjoy the road I'm on. —Deepak Chopra

86. We do not really change over time; we are as flowers unfolding; we merely become more nearly like ourselves. —Anne Rice, *The Queen of the Damned*

87. The most beautiful thing we can experience is the mysterious. It is the source of all true art and science. He to whom this emotion is a stranger, who can

no longer pause to wonder and stand rapt in awe, is as good as dead. —Albert Einstein

88. A cloud does not know why it moves in just such a direction and at such a speed. It feels an impulsion. This is the place to go now. But the sky knows the reasons and the patterns behind all clouds, and you will know, too, when you lift yourself high enough to see beyond horizons. —Richard Bach, *Illusions*

89. Chaos, she decided, that's what love was, or at least what attraction was. Two people, a simple system, but beyond the capacity of the human mind to predict. —Garfield Reeves-Stevens, *Dark Matter*

90. Who, if I cried out, would hear me among the angels' hierarchies? And even if one of them pressed me suddenly against his heart: I would be consumed in that overwhelming existence. For beauty is nothing but the beginning of terror, which we are just able to endure. And we are so awed because it serenely disdains to annihilate us. Every angel is terrifying. —Rainer Maria Rilke

91. In the fractal world, an entire ecosystem can exist in the plumage of a bird. . . . In the real world, where species multiply until halted, space is not measured in ordinary Euclidean dimensions but in fractal dimensions. —Edward O. Wilson, *The Diversity of Life*

92. If we wish to make a new world we have the material ready. The first one, too, was made out of chaos. —Robert Quillen

93. It is as if a large diamond were to be found inside each person. Picture a diamond a foot long. The diamond has a thousand facets, but the facets are covered with dirt and tar. It is the job of the soul to clean each facet until the surface is brilliant and can reflect a rainbow of colors.
—Brian Weiss, M.D., *Many Lives, Many Masters*

94. We are like the explorers of a great continent who have penetrated to its margins in most points of the compass and have mapped the major mountain chains and rivers. There are still innumerable details to fill in, but the endless horizons no longer exist.
—Bentley Glass

95. Laws of physics and mathematics are like a coordinate system that runs in only one dimension. Perhaps there is another dimension perpendicular to it, invisible to those laws of physics, describing the same things with different rules, and those rules are written in our hearts, in a deep place where we cannot go and read them except in our dreams.
—Neal Stephenson, *The Diamond Age*

96. When you are seventy years old and look back at what your life has meant, you will not focus on your solo activities. What you will remember are the incidents of touching, those times when your life was enriched by a moment of sharing with a friend or loved one. It is our mutual awareness of this miracle called life that allows us to accept our mortality.
—Arthur C. Clarke and Gentry Lee, *Cradle*

97. A lasting relationship with a woman is only possible if you are a business failure. —Billionaire J. Paul Getty, married and divorced five times, in a *Time* article about how women are attracted to men with power and money.

98. In a universe divested of illusions and lights, man feels an alien, a stranger. His exile is without remedy since he is deprived of the memory of a lost home or the hope of a promised land. —Albert Camus

99. High up in the North in the land called Svithjod, there stands a rock. It is a hundred miles high and a hundred miles wide. Once every thousand years a little bird comes to the rock to sharpen its beak. When the rock has thus been worn away, then a single day of eternity will have gone by.
—Hendrik Willem van Loon, *The Story of Mankind*

100. You do not need to leave your room. Remain sitting at your table and listen. Do not even listen, simply wait. Do not even wait, be quite still and solitary. The world will freely offer itself to you to be unmasked, it has no choice, it will roll in ecstasy at your feet. —Franz Kafka

ABOUT THE AUTHOR

Clifford A. Pickover graduated first in his class from Franklin and Marshall College, after completing the four-year undergraduate program in three years. He went on to receive his Ph.D. from Yale University's Department of Molecular Biophysics and Biochemistry. Dr. Pickover's primary interest is finding new ways to expand creativity by melding art, science, mathematics, and other seemingly disparate areas of human endeavor. A prolific author, Pickover "has published nearly a book a year in which he stretches the limits of computers, art and thought," as the *Los Angeles Times* noted recently. His many books have been translated into Italian, German, Japanese, Chinese, Korean, Portuguese, and Polish. Among his works for popular audiences are *The Girl Who Gave Birth to Rabbits* (Prometheus, 2000), *Surfing through Hyperspace* (Oxford University Press, 1999), *Wonders of Numbers* ⊗ (Oxford University Press, 2001), *The Science of Aliens* (Basic Books, 1998), *Time: A Traveler's Guide* (Oxford University Press, 1998), *Strange Brains and Genius: The Secret Lives of Eccentric Scientists and Madmen* (Plenum, 1998), *The Alien IQ Test* (Basic Books, 1997), *The Loom of God* ॐ (Plenum, 1997), *Black Holes: A Traveler's Guide* ✸ (Wiley, 1996), and *Keys to Infinity* ☯ (Wiley, 1995). He has written numerous other highly acclaimed books, including *Chaos in Wonderland: Visual Adventures in a Fractal World* (1994), *Mazes for the Mind: Computers and the Unexpected* (1992), *Computers and the Imagination* (1991), and *Computers, Pattern, Chaos, and Beauty* (1990), all published by St. Martin's Press, and more than two hundred articles concerning science, art, and mathematics. He is also coauthor, with Piers Anthony, of *Spider Legs*, a novel recently listed by Barnes and Noble as its second-best-selling science fiction title.

Dr. Pickover is currently an associate editor for the scientific journal *Computers and Graphics* and is an editorial board member for *Theta Mathematics Journal*, *Odyssey*, *Idealistic Studies*, *Leonardo*, and *YLEM*. He has been a guest editor for several scientific journals and the associate editor of *Computers in Physics* and *Speculations in Science and Technology*.

He has served as editor of the books *Chaos and Fractals: A Computer Graphical Journey* (Elsevier, 1998), *The Pattern Book: Fractals, Art, and Nature* (World Scientific, 1995), *Visions of the Future: Art, Technology, and Computing in the Next Century* (St. Martin's Press, 1993), *Future Health: Computers and Medicine in the Twenty-first Century* (St. Martin's Press, 1995), *Fractal Horizons: The Future Use of Fractals* (St. Martin's Press, 1996), and *Visualizing Biological Information* (World Scientific, 1995). He was coeditor of the books *Spiral Symmetry* (World Scientific, 1992) and *Frontiers of Scientific Visualization* (Wiley, 1994).

Pickover received first prize in the Institute of Physics "Beauty of Physics Photographic Competition," and his computer graphics have been featured on the covers of many popular magazines. His research has received considerable attention by the press—including CNN's "Science and Technology Week," the Discovery Channel, *Science News*, the *Washington Post*, *Wired*, and the *Christian Science Monitor*—and his work has been included in international exhibitions and museums. *OMNI* magazine has described him as "Van Leeuwenhoek's twentieth-century equivalent." *Scientific American* has several times featured his graphic work, calling it "strange and beautiful, stunningly realistic." *Wired* wrote, "Bucky Fuller thought big, Arthur C. Clarke thinks big, but Cliff Pickover outdoes them both." Among the many patents Pickover has received are those for a 3-D computer mouse, for strange computer icons, and for black-hole transporter interfaces to computers.

Dr. Pickover is currently a research staff member at the IBM T. J. Watson Research Center, where he has received seventeen invention achievement awards, three research division awards, and four external honor awards. He is the "Brain-Strain" columnist for *Odyssey* magazine and for many years was the "Brain-Boggler" columnist for *Discover* magazine.

Dr. Pickover's hobbies include the practice of Ch'ang-Shih t'ai chi ch'uan and Shaolin kung fu, raising golden and green severums (large Amazonian fish), and piano playing (mostly jazz). He is a member of the SETI League, a group of signal processing enthusiasts who systematically search the universe for intelligent, extraterrestrial life. His website, http://www.pickover.com, has received over 200,000 visits. He can be reached there or at P.O. Box 549, Millwood, New York 10546-0549, USA.

designed by George Bain, with acknowledgements to an unknown artist of the Book of Lindisfarne

Gum biodh Eòin Graidh nan Gaidheal
Fillte ri dealbh do bheatha.

May the Birds of Friendship of the Gael be ever woven into the web of your life.

Works by Clifford A. Pickover

The Alien IQ Test
Black Holes: A Traveler's Guide
Chaos and Fractals
Chaos in Wonderland: Visual Adventures in a Fractal World
Computers, Pattern, Chaos, and Beauty
Computers and the Imagination
Fractal Horizons: The Future Use of Fractals
Frontiers of Scientific Visualization (with Stu Tewksbury)
Future Health: Computers and Medicine in the Twenty-first Century
The Girl Who Gave Birth to Rabbits
Keys to Infinity
The Loom of God
Mazes for the Mind: Computers and the Unexpected
The Pattern Book: Fractals, Art, and Nature
The Science of Aliens
Spider Legs (with Piers Anthony)
Spiral Symmetry (with Istvan Hargittai)
Strange Brains and Genius
Surfing through Hyperspace
Time: A Traveler's Guide
Visions of the Future: Art, Technology, and Computing in the Next Century
Visualizing Biological Information
Wonders of Numbers